IT'S STILL A MOM'S LIFE

IT'S STILL A MOM'S LIFE

by

David Sipress

A PLUME BOOK

PLUME
Published by the Penguin Group
Penguin Books USA Inc., 375 Hudson Street, New York, New York 10014, U.S.A.
Penguin Books Ltd, 27 Wrights Lane, London W8 5TZ, England
Penguin Books Australia Ltd, Ringwood, Victoria, Australia
Penguin Books Canada Ltd, 10 Alcorn Avenue, Toronto, Ontario, Canada M4V 3B2
Penguin Books (N.Z.) Ltd, 182–190 Wairau Road, Auckland 10, New Zealand

Penguin Books Ltd, Registered Offices: Harmondsworth, Middlesex, England

First published by Plume, an imprint of New American Library,
a division of Penguin Books USA Inc.

First Printing, May, 1993
10 9 8 7 6 5 4 3 2 1

Some of these cartoons appeared in *Parenting* and *Children's Television Workshop Parents' Guide.*

 REGISTERED TRADEMARK—MARCA REGISTRADA

LIBRARY OF CONGRESS CATALOGING-IN-PUBLICATION DATA
Sipress, David.
  It's still a mom's life / David Sipress.
  ISBN 0-452-26867-2
  1. Motherhood—Caricatures and cartoons.   2. American wit and
humor, Pictorial.   I. Title.
NC1429.S532A4   1993   92-44483
741.5'973—dc20   CIP

Printed in the United States of America

BOOKS ARE AVAILABLE AT QUANTITY DISCOUNTS WHEN USED TO PROMOTE PRODUCTS OR SERVICES.
FOR INFORMATION PLEASE WRITE TO PREMIUM MARKETING DIVISION, PENGUIN BOOKS USA INC., 375 HUDSON STREET, NEW YORK, NEW YORK 10014.

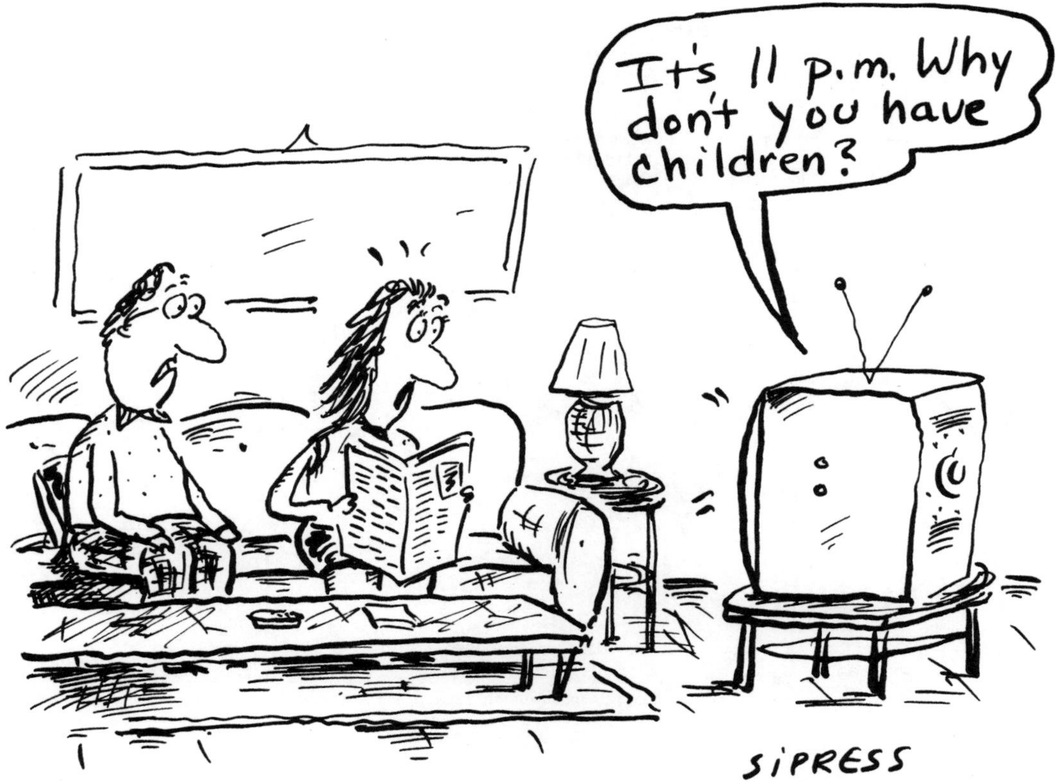
It's 11 p.m. Why don't you have children?
SIPRESS

1
Im afraid that when I have a baby I'll lose my freedom, my leisure time, my career and my security. What are you afraid of?
2
Stretch marks.
SIPRESS

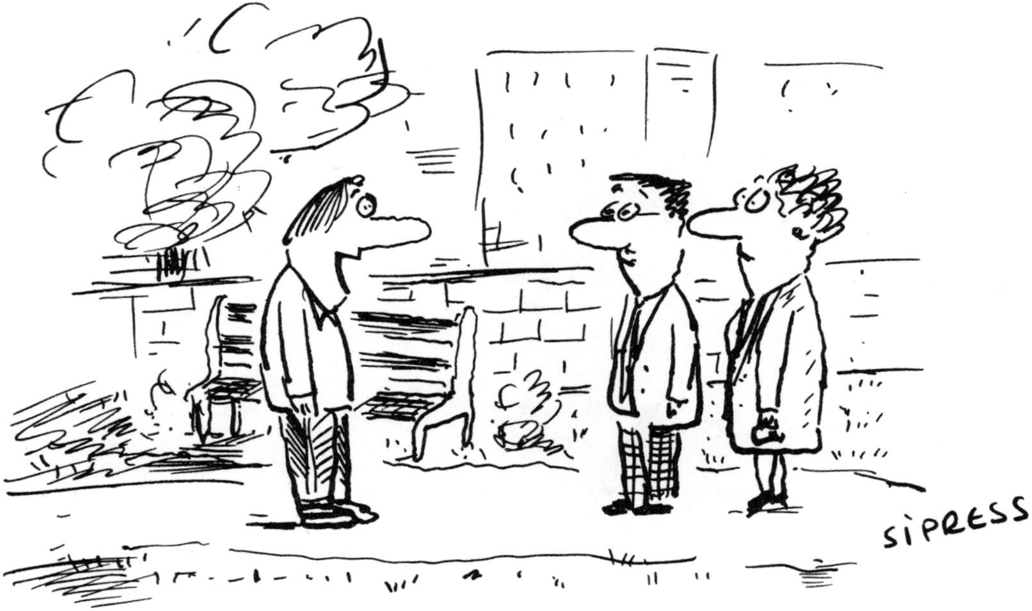
SIPRESS

We're pregnant, but only one of us is too sick to get out of bed.

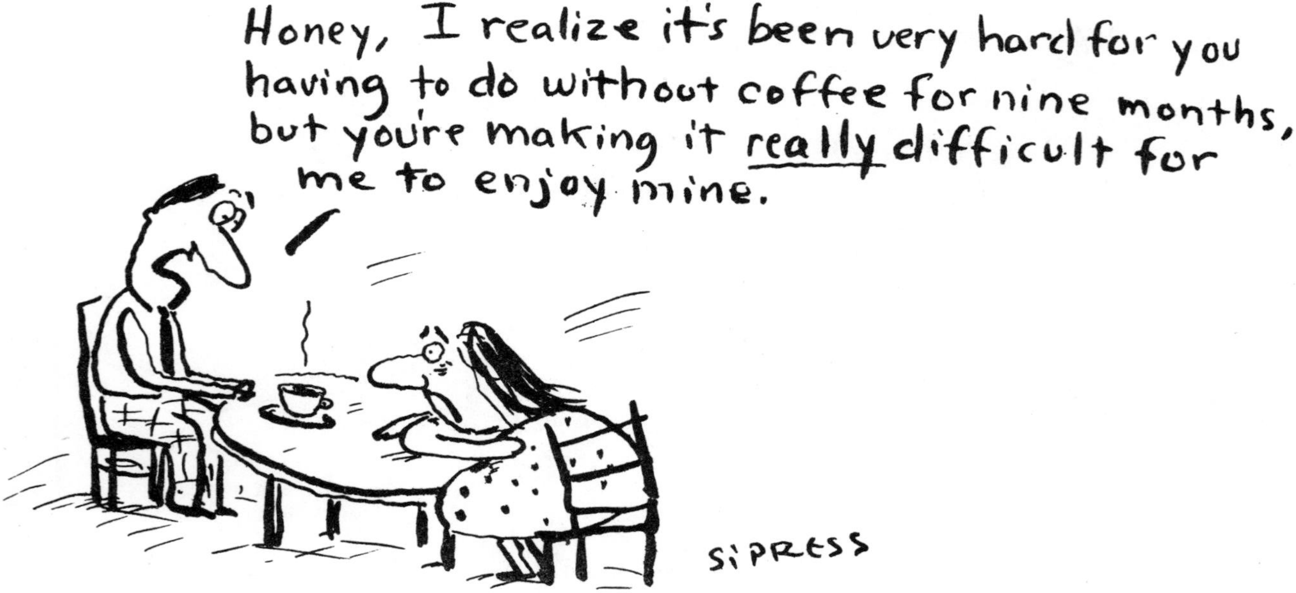
Honey, I realize it's been very hard for you having to do without coffee for nine months, but you're making it *really* difficult for me to enjoy mine.
SIPRESS

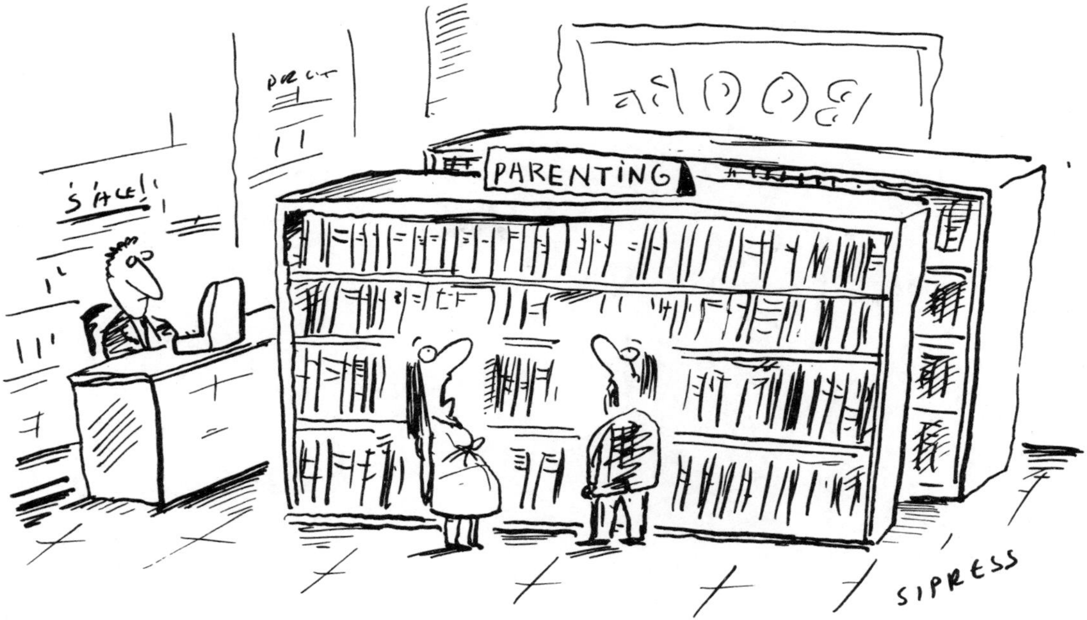
PARENTING
SIPRESS

How in the world are we going to read them all by July??

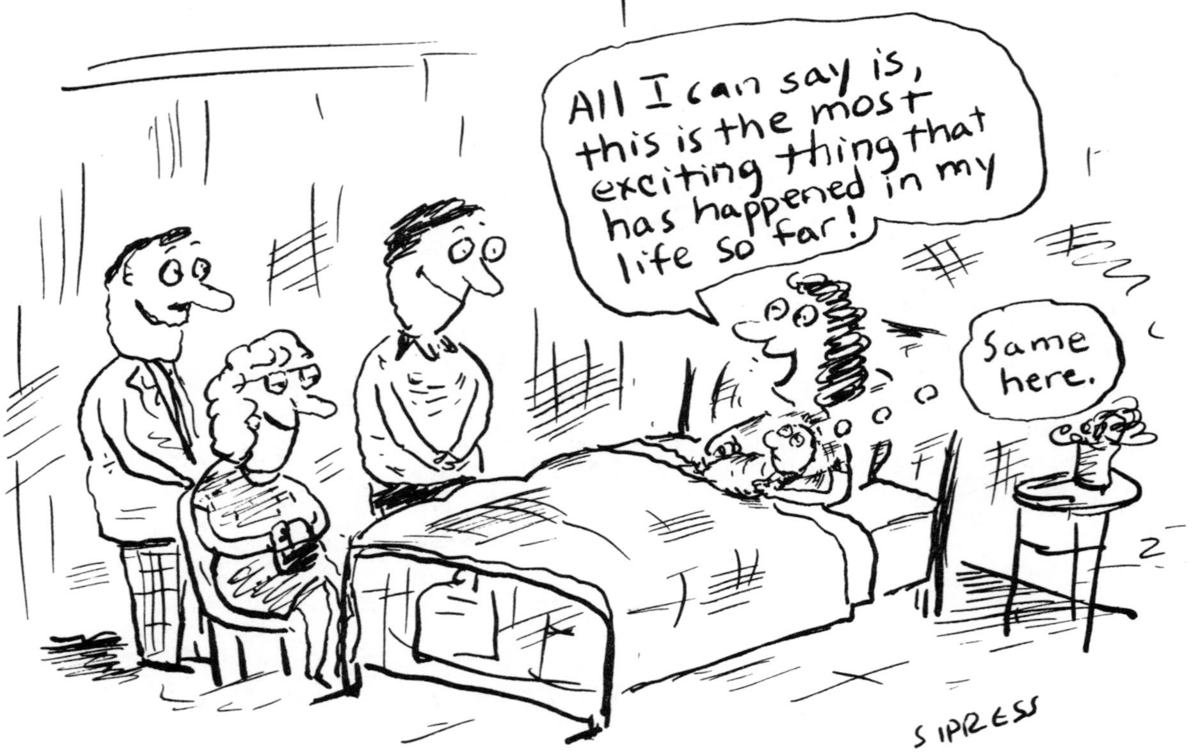
All I can say is, this is the most exciting thing that has happened in my life so far!
Same here.
SIPRESS

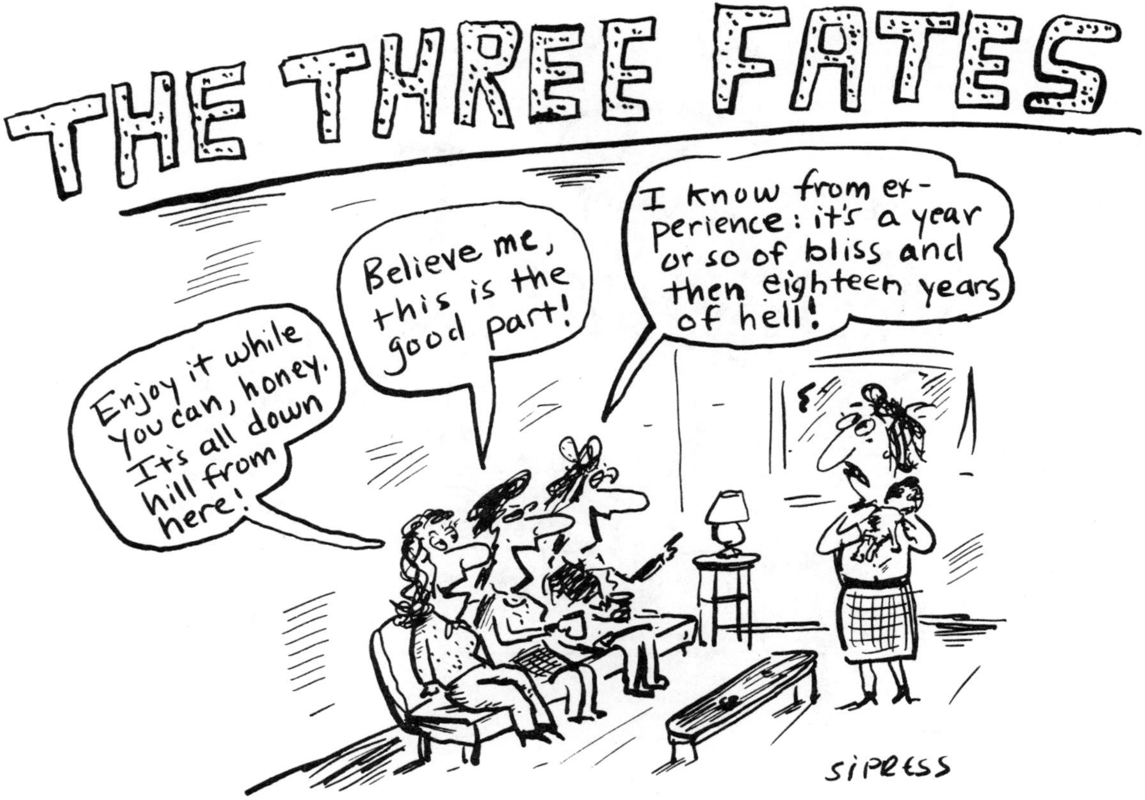
THE THREE FATES
Enjoy it while you can, honey. It's all downhill from here!
Believe me, this is the good part!
I know from experience: it's a year or so of bliss and then eighteen years of hell!
SIPRESS

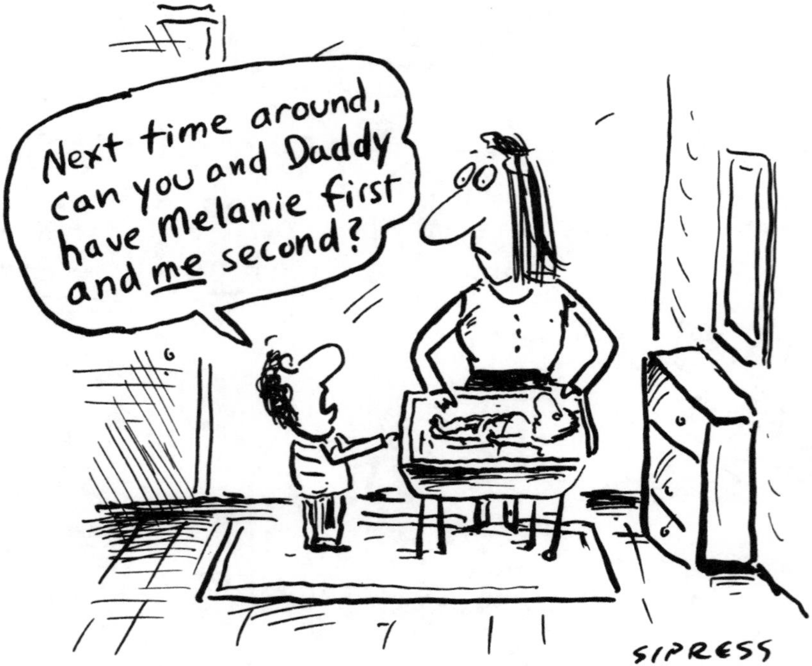
Next time around, can you and Daddy have Melanie first and me second?
SIPRESS

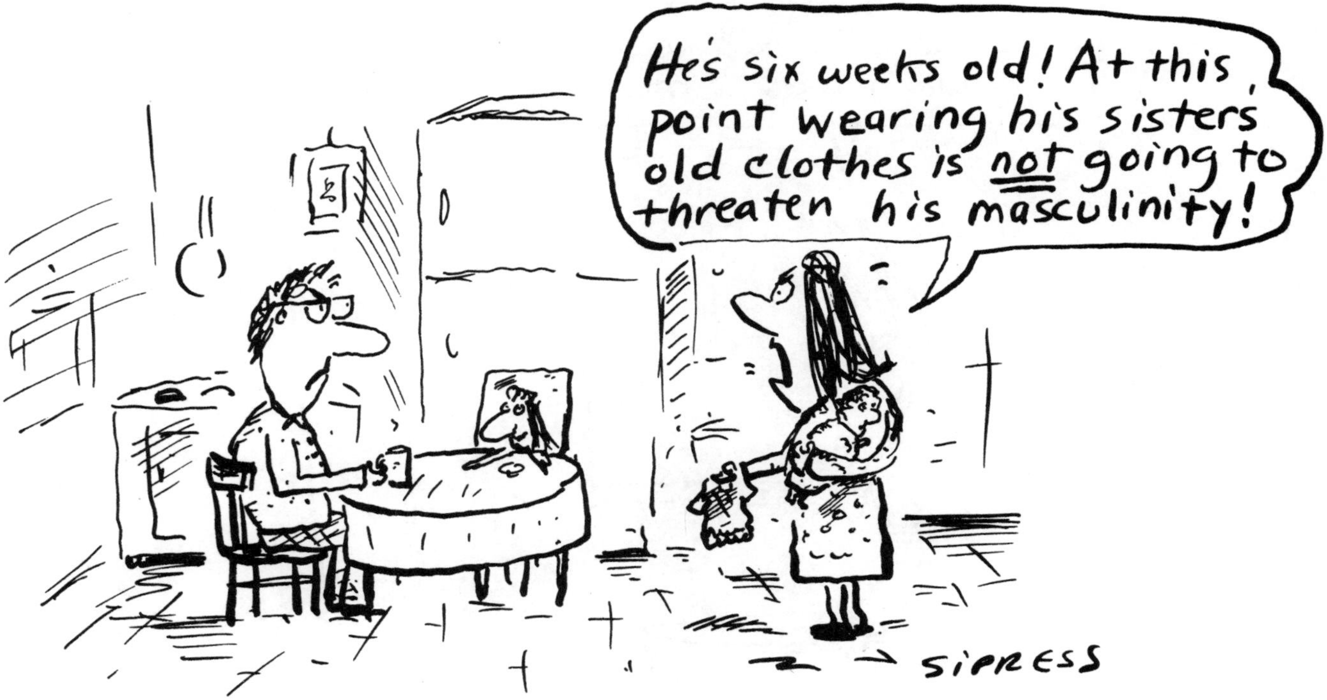
He's six weeks old! At this point wearing his sister's old clothes is not going to threaten his masculinity!
SIPRESS

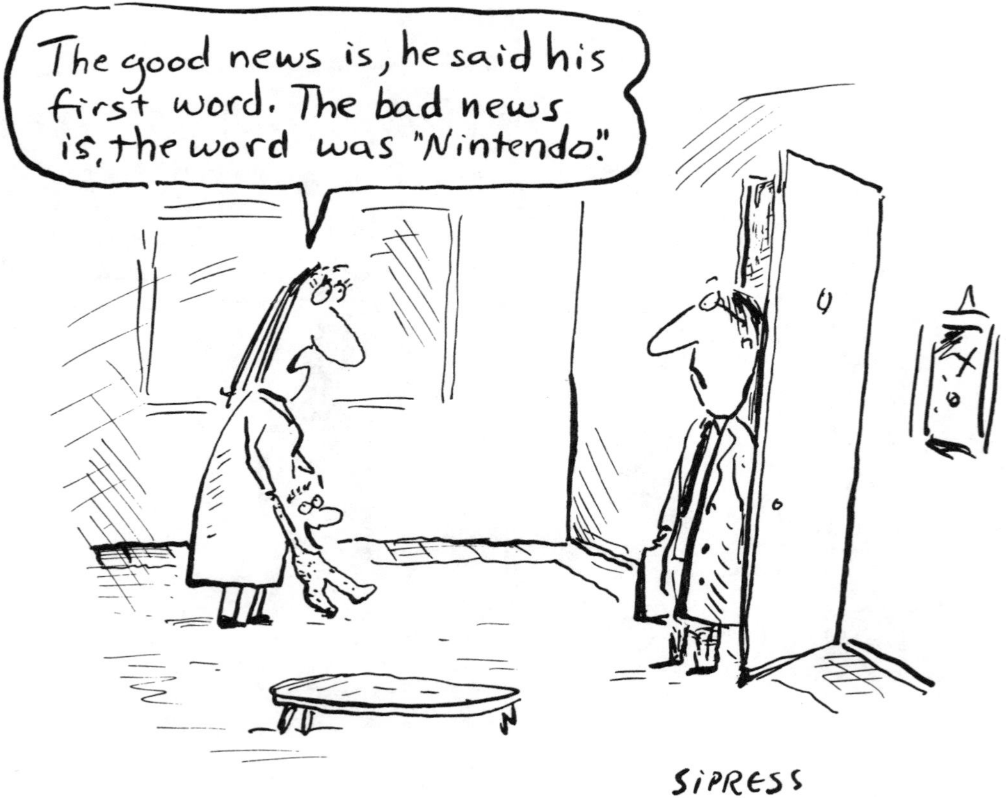
The good news is, he said his first word. The bad news is, the word was "Nintendo."
SIPRESS

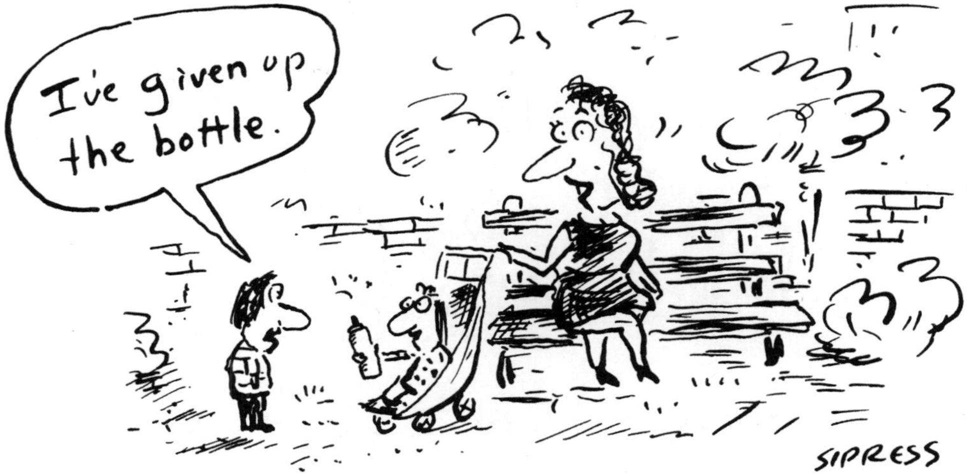
I've given up the bottle.
SIPRESS

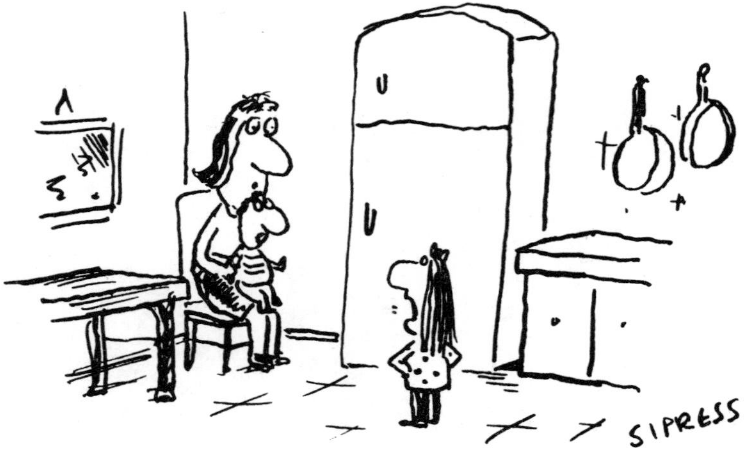
SIPRESS

Yesterday you said *I* was the best kid in the whole world. Today I hear you telling Billy that he is. Now, which is it Mom???

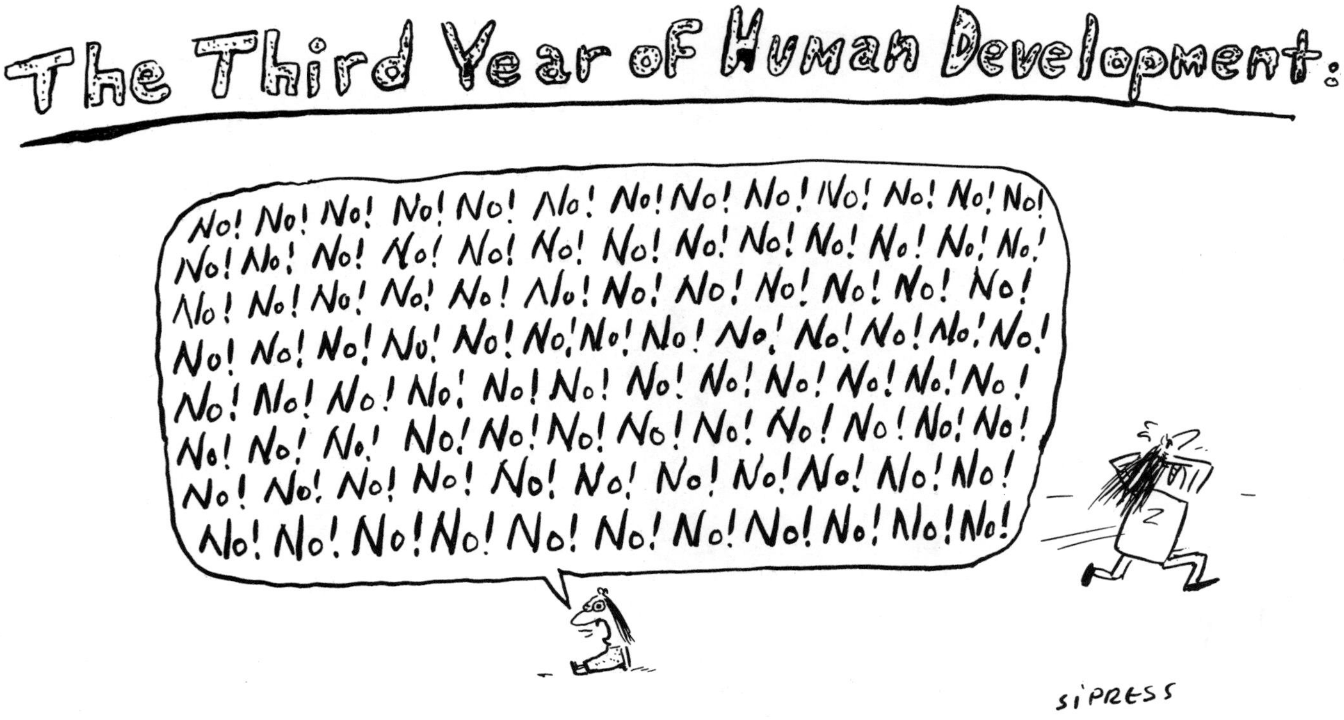
The Third Year of Human Development:
No! No! No! No! No! No! No! No! No! No! No! No! No! No! No! No! No! No! No! No! No! No! No! No! No! No! No! No! No! No! No! No! No! No! No! No! No! No! No! No! No! No! No! No! No! No! No! No! No! No! No! No! No! No! No! No! No! No! No! No! No! No! No! No! No! No! No! No! No! No! No! No! No! No! No! No! No! No! No! No! No! No! No! No! No! No! No! No! No! No! No! No! No! No! No! No!
SIPRESS

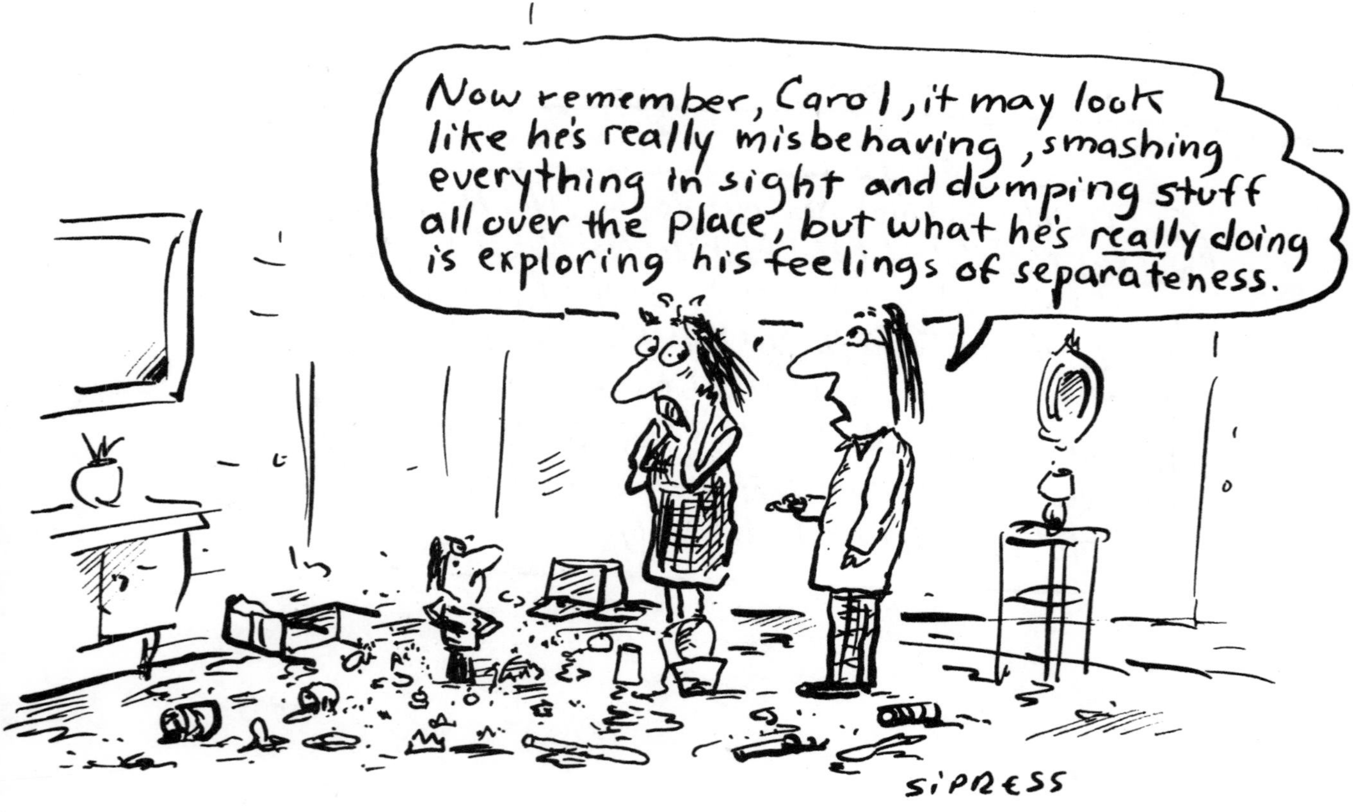
Now remember, Carol, it may look like he's really misbehaving, smashing everything in sight and dumping stuff all over the place, but what he's really doing is exploring his feelings of separateness.
SIPRESS

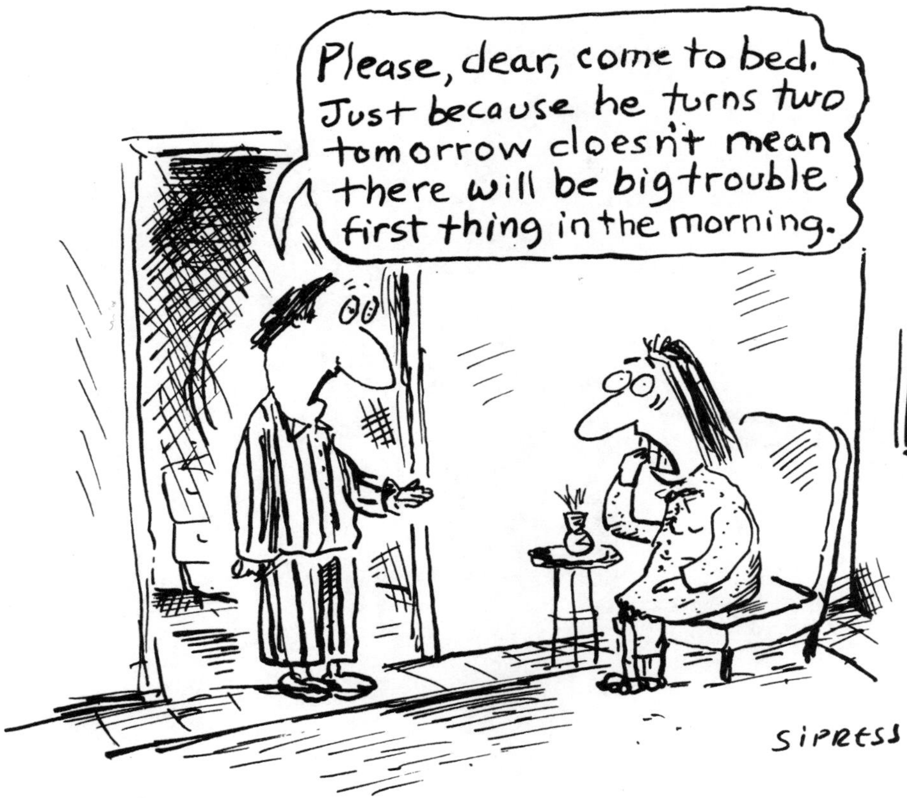
Please, dear, come to bed. Just because he turns two tomorrow doesn't mean there will be big trouble first thing in the morning.
SIPRESS

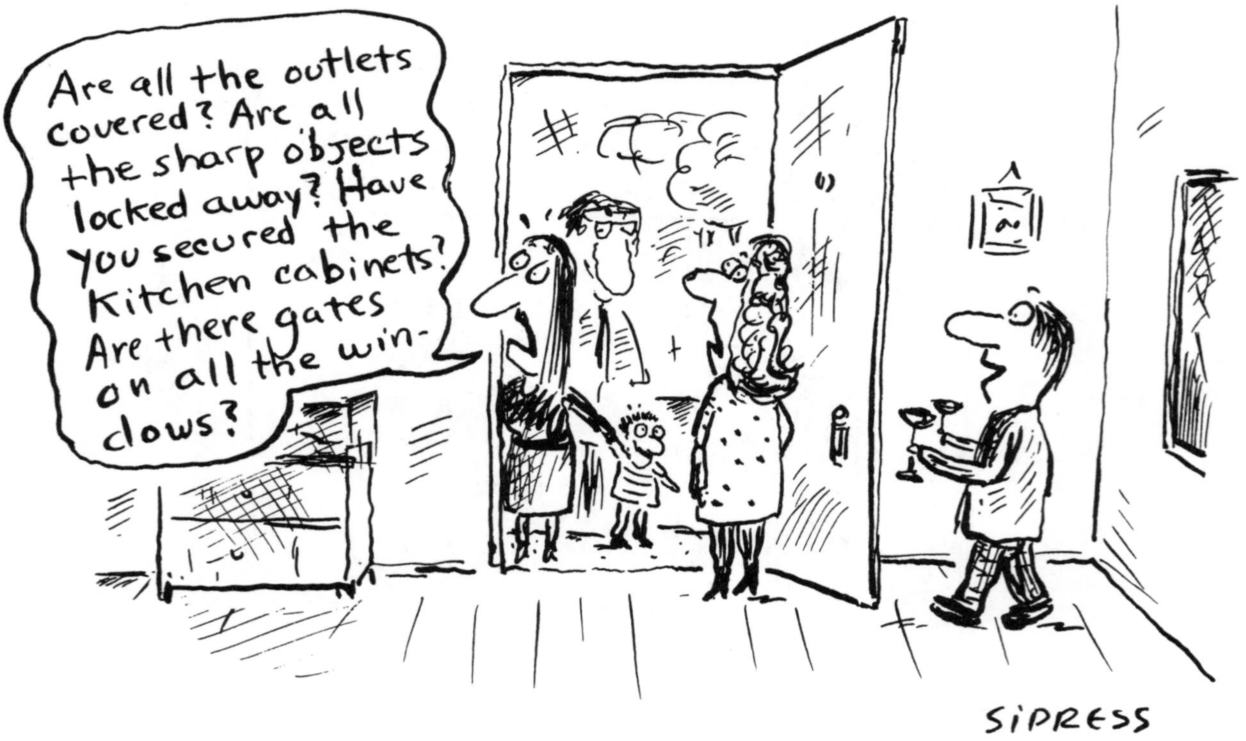

Are all the outlets covered? Are all the sharp objects locked away? Have you secured the kitchen cabinets? Are there gates on all the windows?
SIPRESS

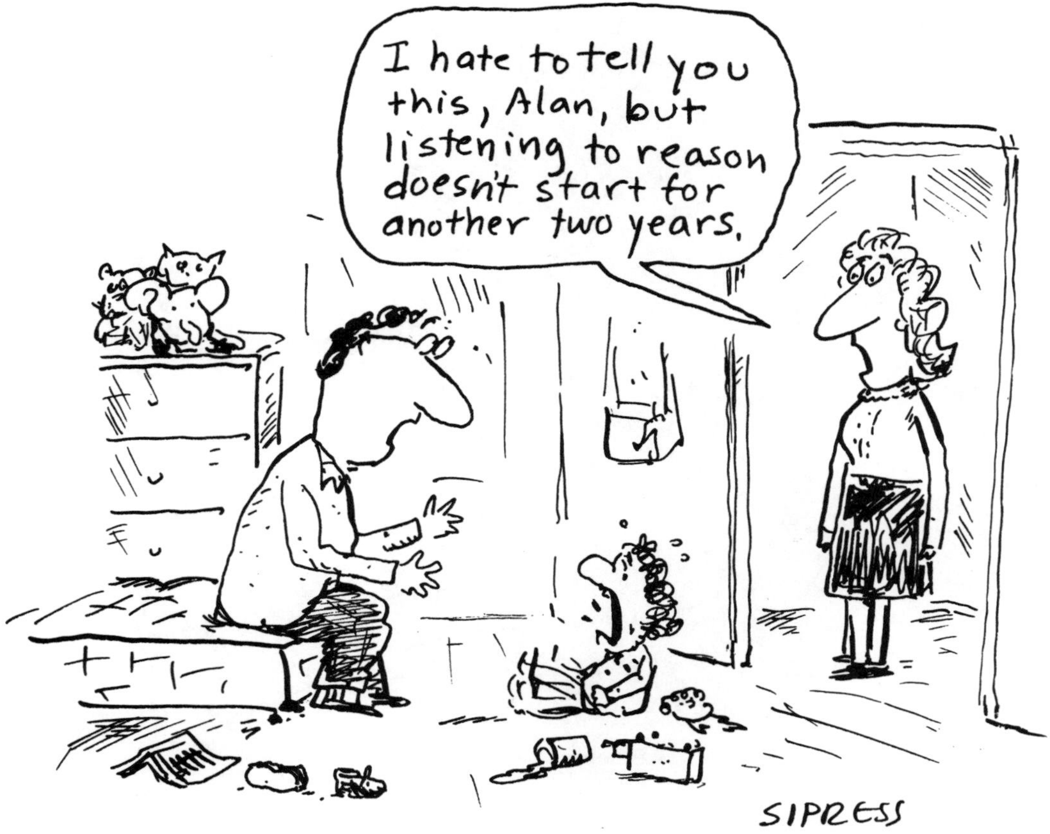
I hate to tell you this, Alan, but listening to reason doesn't start for another two years.
SIPRESS

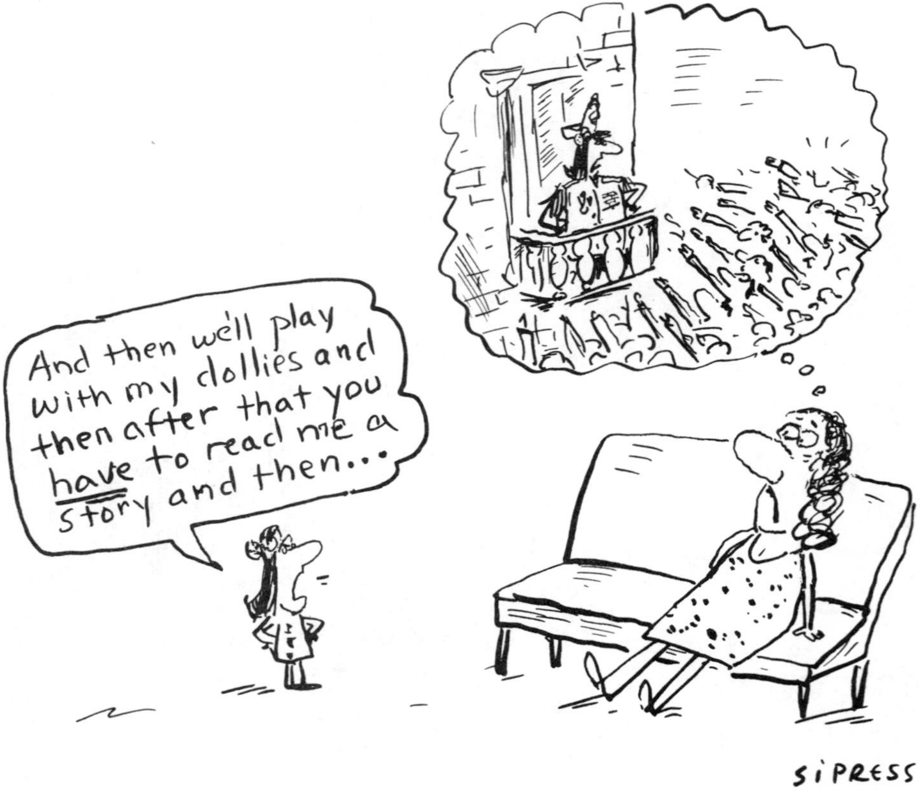
And then we'll play with my dollies and then after that you have to read me a story and then...
SIPRESS

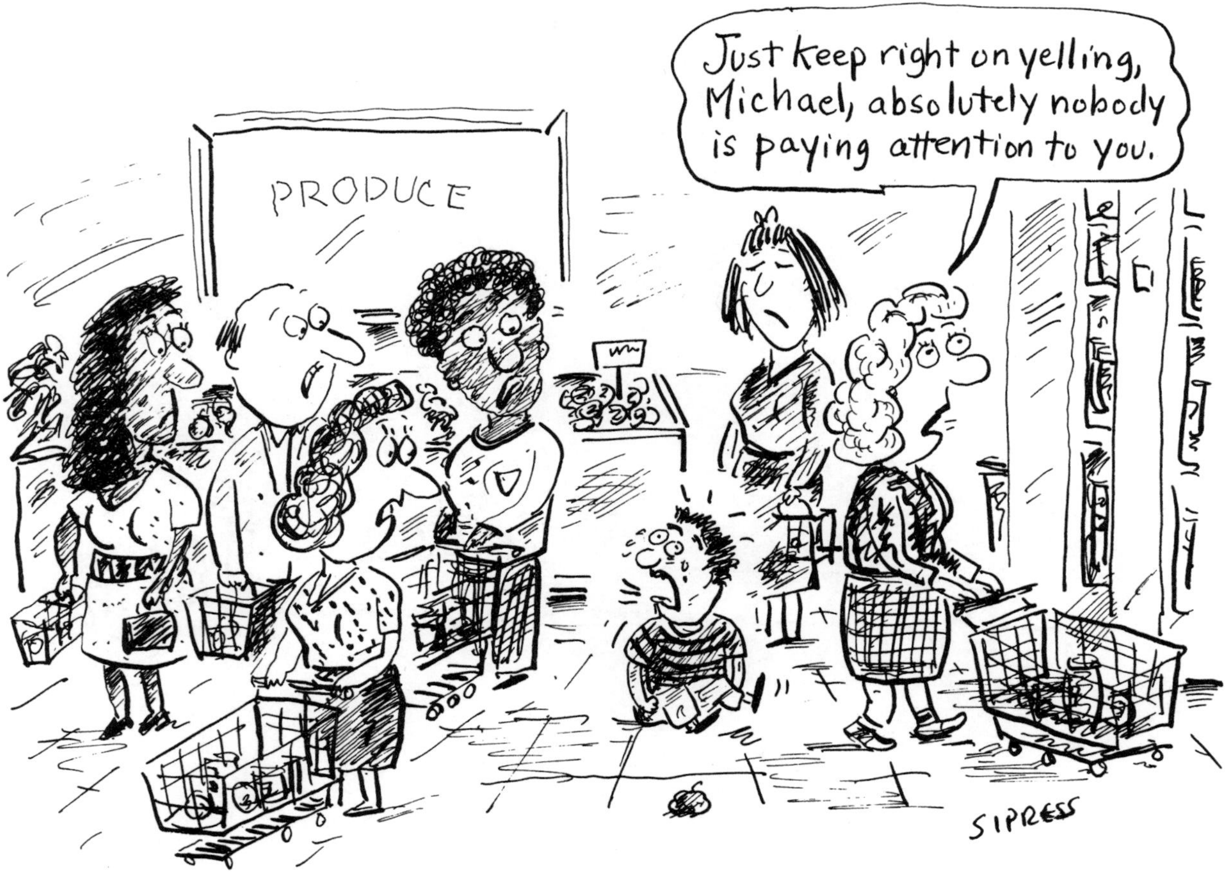
Just keep right on yelling, Michael, absolutely nobody is paying attention to you.
PRODUCE
SIPRESS

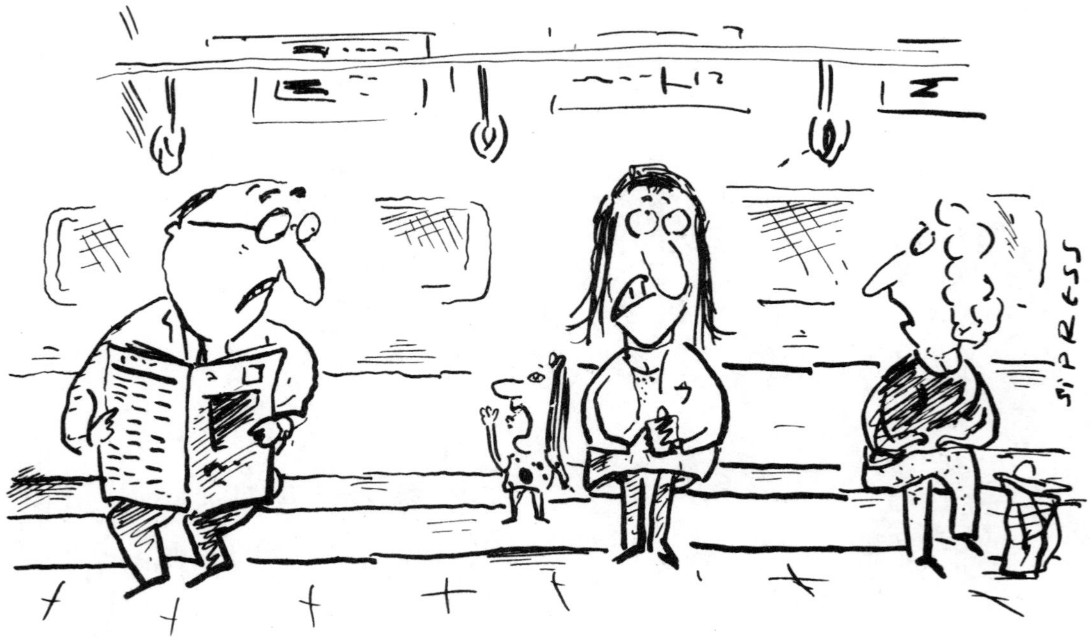
SIPRESS

Hi, stinky doody head!

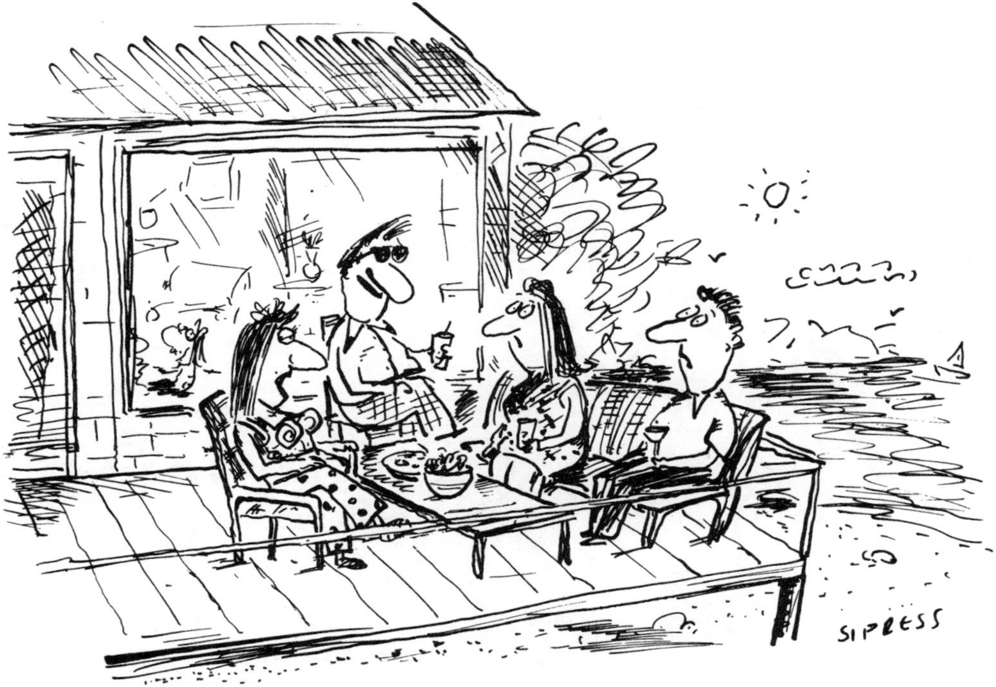
SIPRESS

Right now we're trying to decide between another baby and a B.M.W.

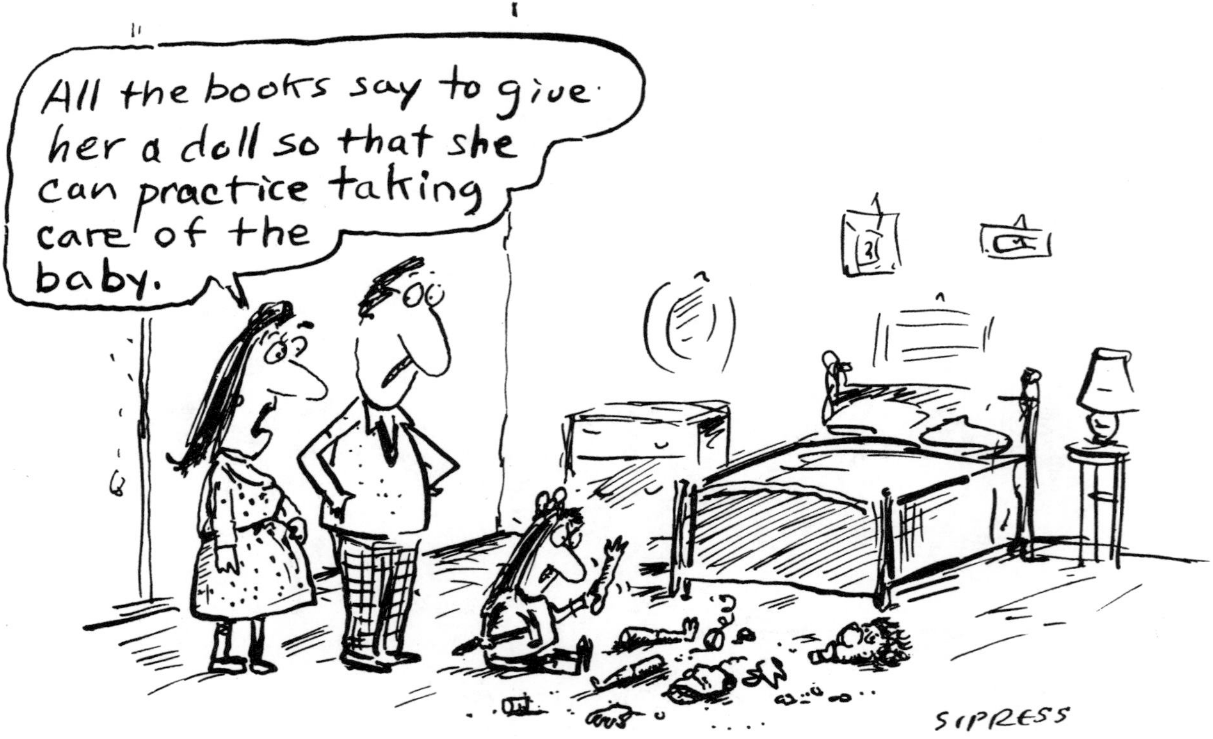
All the books say to give her a doll so that she can practice taking care of the baby.
SIPRESS

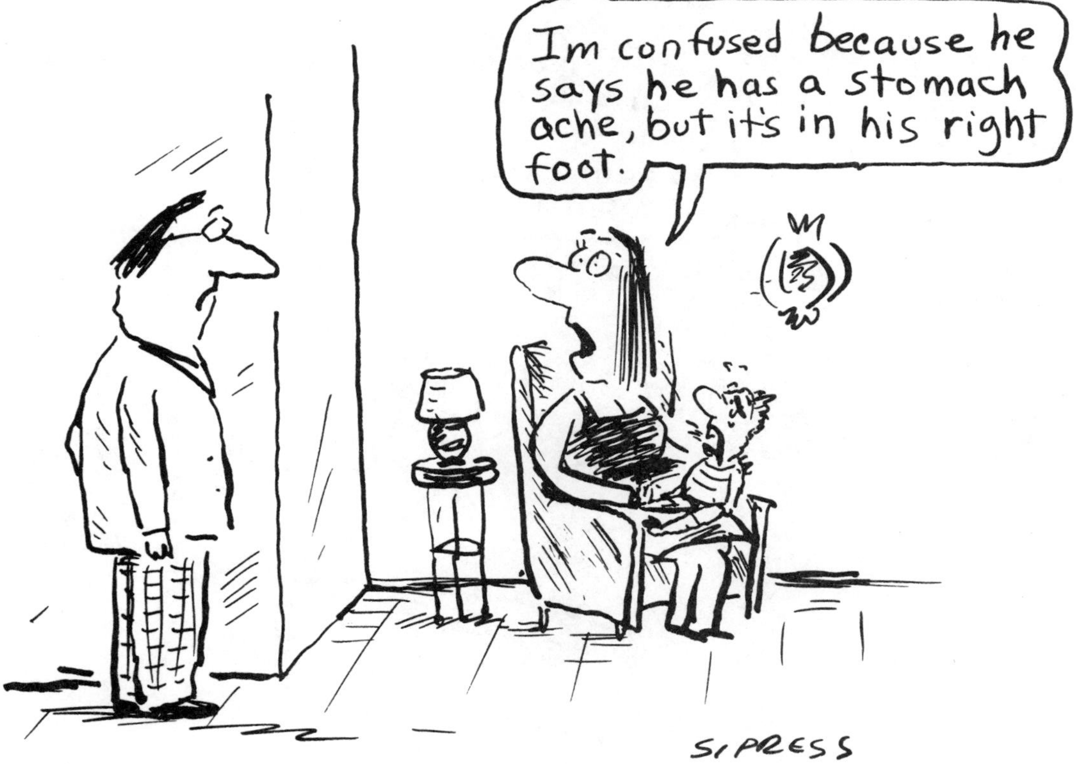
Im confused because he says he has a stomach ache, but it's in his right foot.
SIPRESS

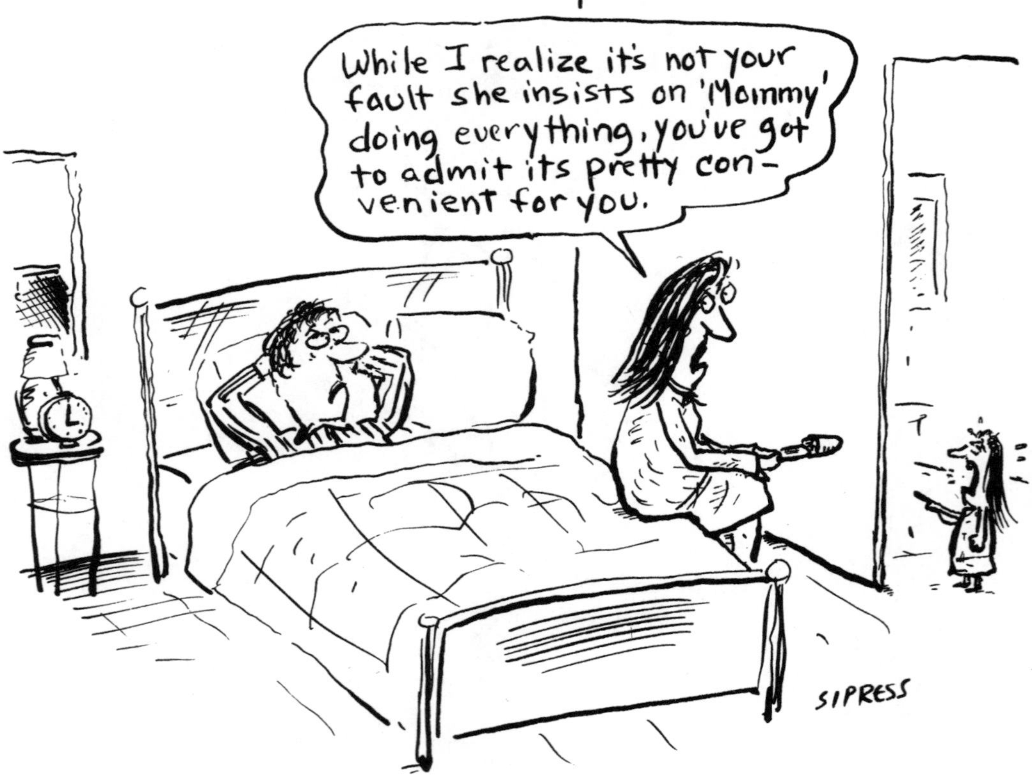
While I realize it's not your fault she insists on 'Mommy' doing everything, you've got to admit its pretty convenient for you.
SIPRESS

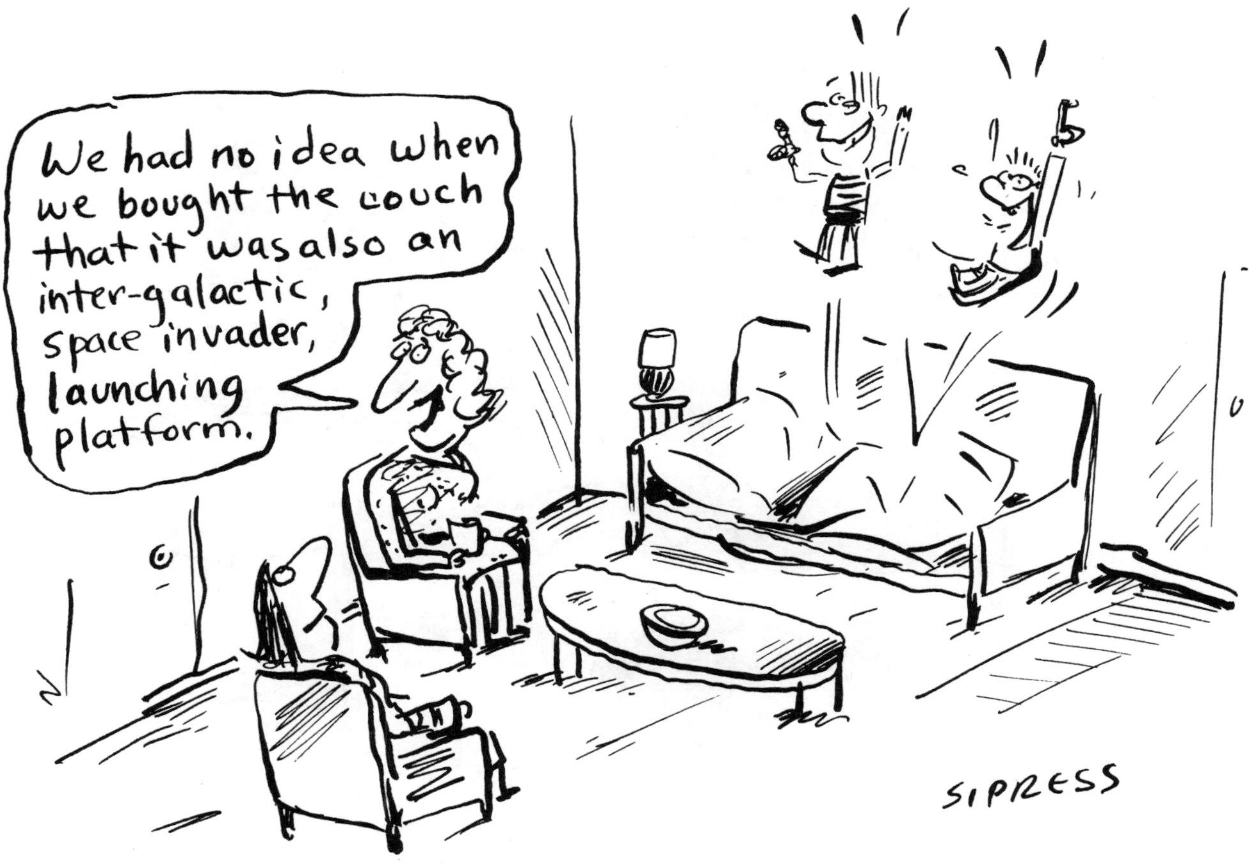
We had no idea when we bought the couch that it was also an inter-galactic, space invader, launching platform.
SIPRESS

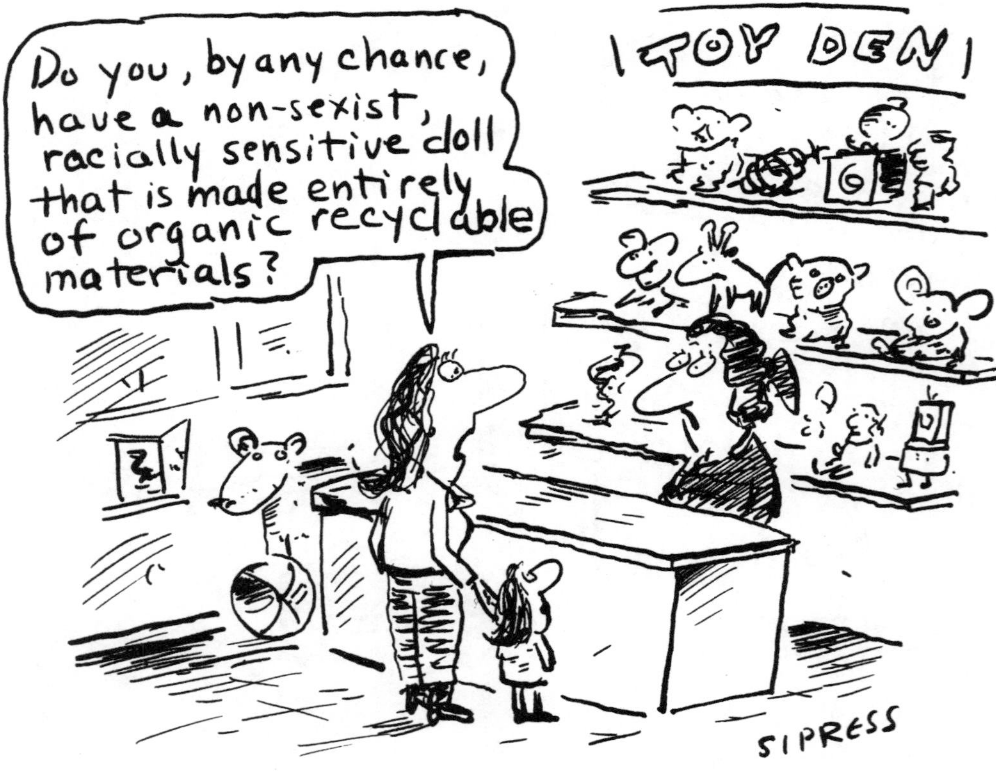
Do you, by any chance, have a non-sexist, racially sensitive doll that is made entirely of organic recyclable materials?
TOY DEN
SIPRESS

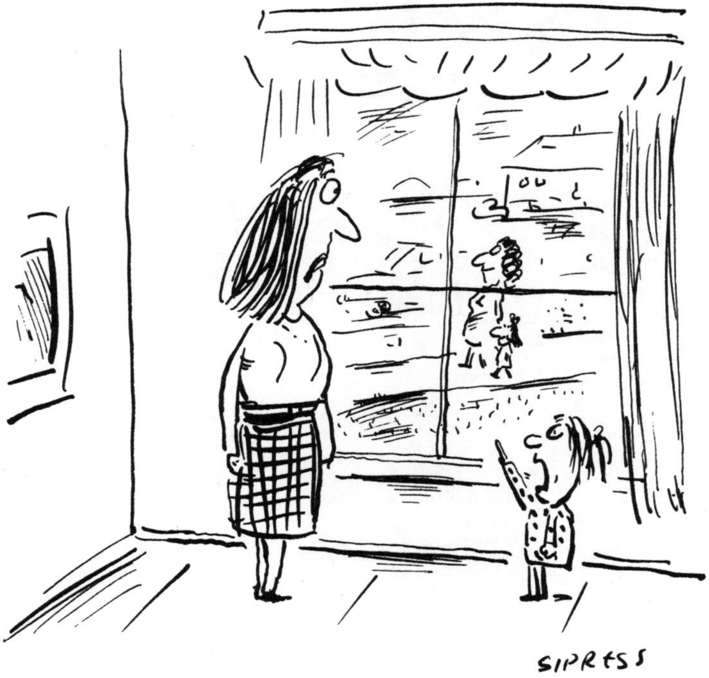
SIPRESS

If it's naptime, how come *that* little girl is still awake??

ANIMAL MOMS

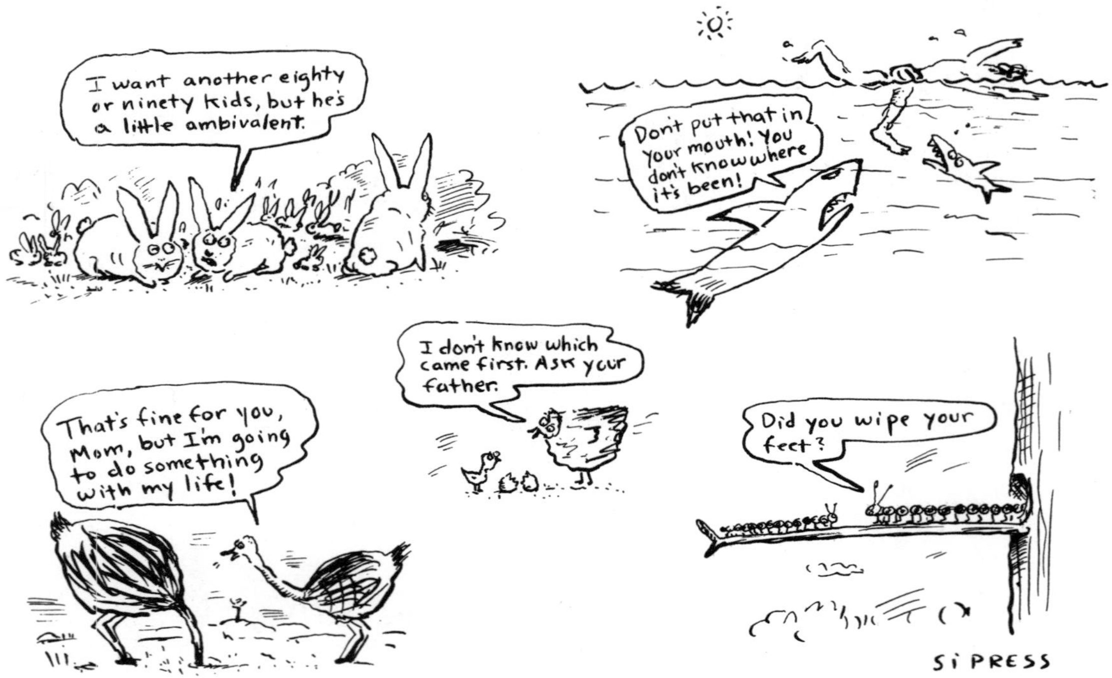

I want another eighty or ninety kids, but he's a little ambivalent.
Don't put that in your mouth! You don't know where it's been!
I don't know which came first. Ask your father.
That's fine for you, Mom, but I'm going to do something with my life!
Did you wipe your feet?
SIPRESS

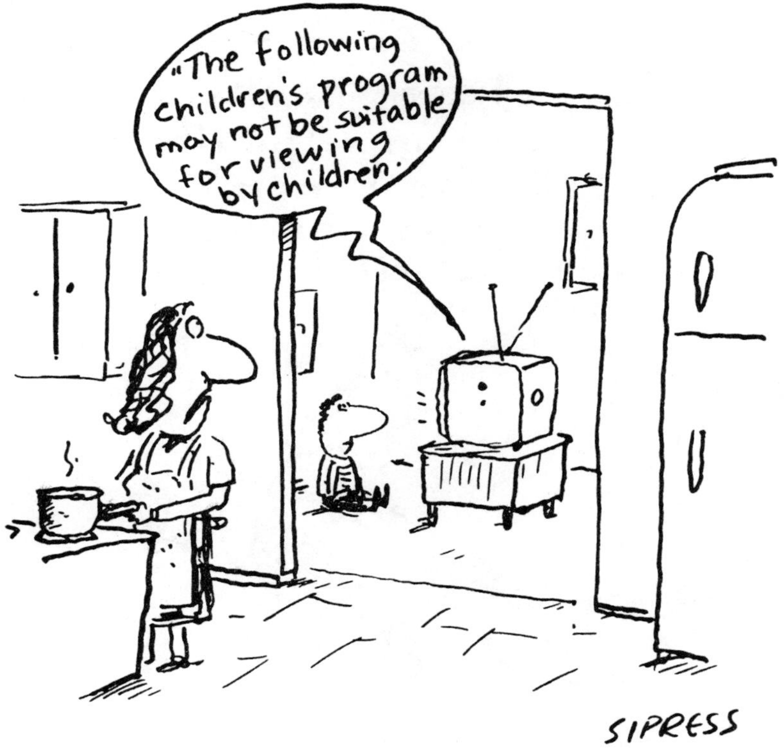
"The following children's program may not be suitable for viewing by children."
SIPRESS

I'm sorry, sweetheart, but if Mommy has to listen to the music from "We Sing in Sillyville" one more time she'll lose her mind and then you won't have anybody to rent you any videos at all!

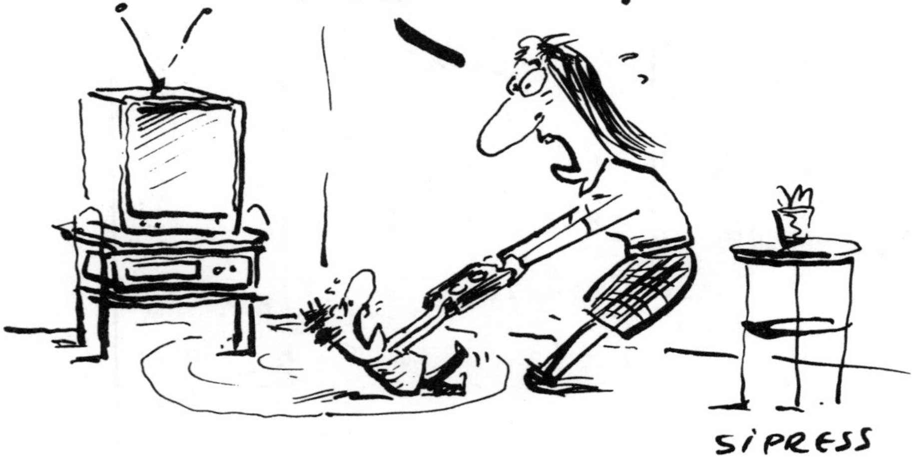
SIPRESS

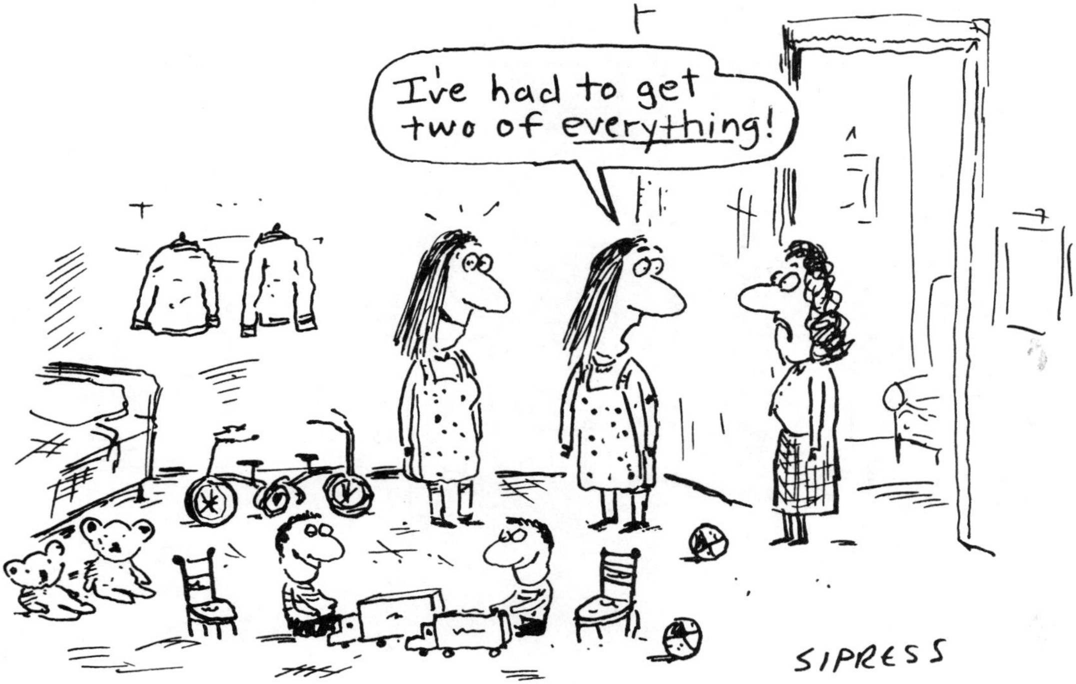
I've had to get two of everything!
SIPRESS

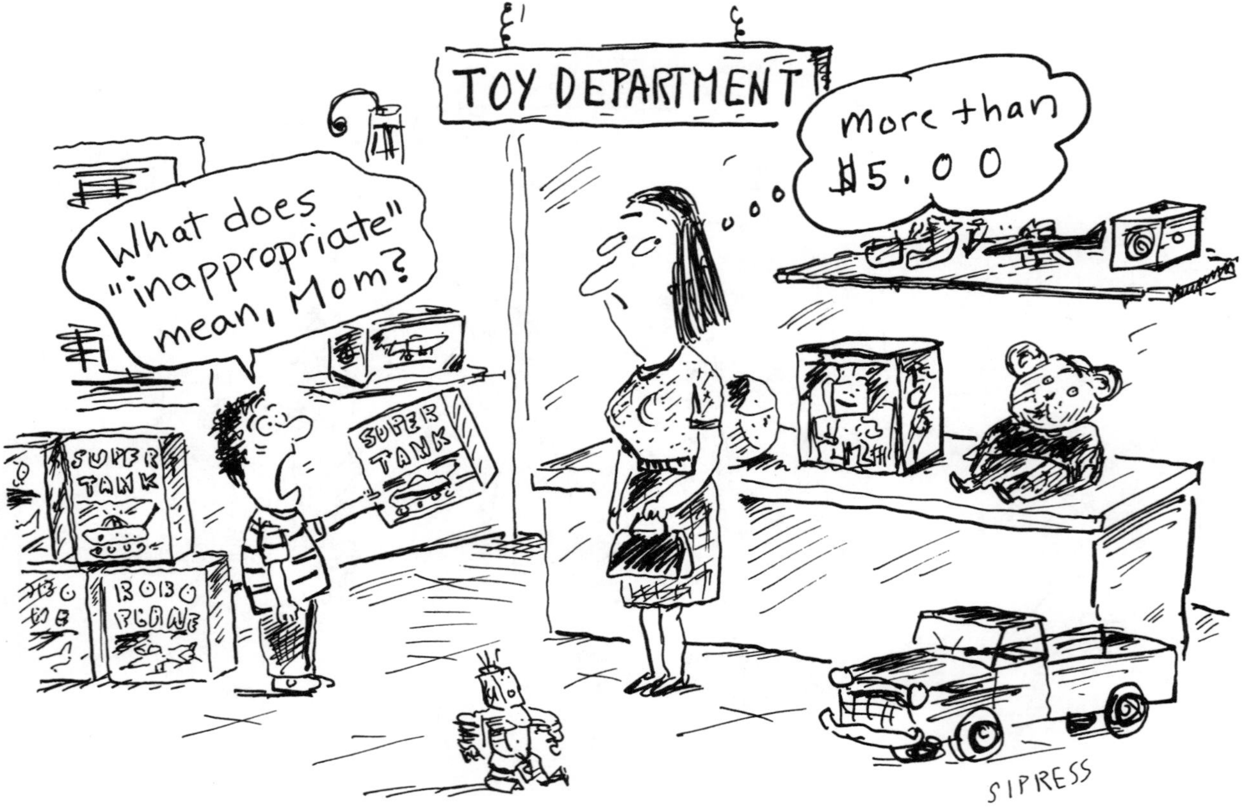

TOY DEPARTMENT
What does "inappropriate" mean, Mom?
More than $5.00
SUPER TANK
SUPER TANK
ROBO PLANE
SIPRESS

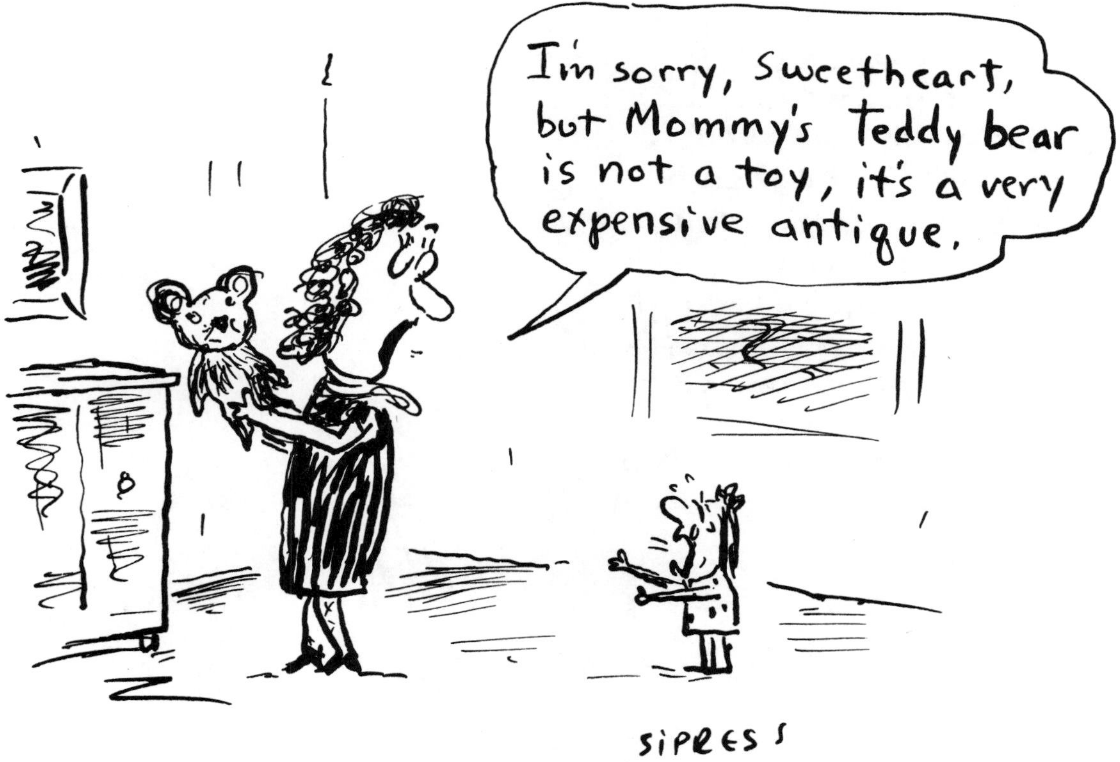
I'm sorry, Sweetheart, but Mommy's teddy bear is not a toy, it's a very expensive antique.
SIPRESS

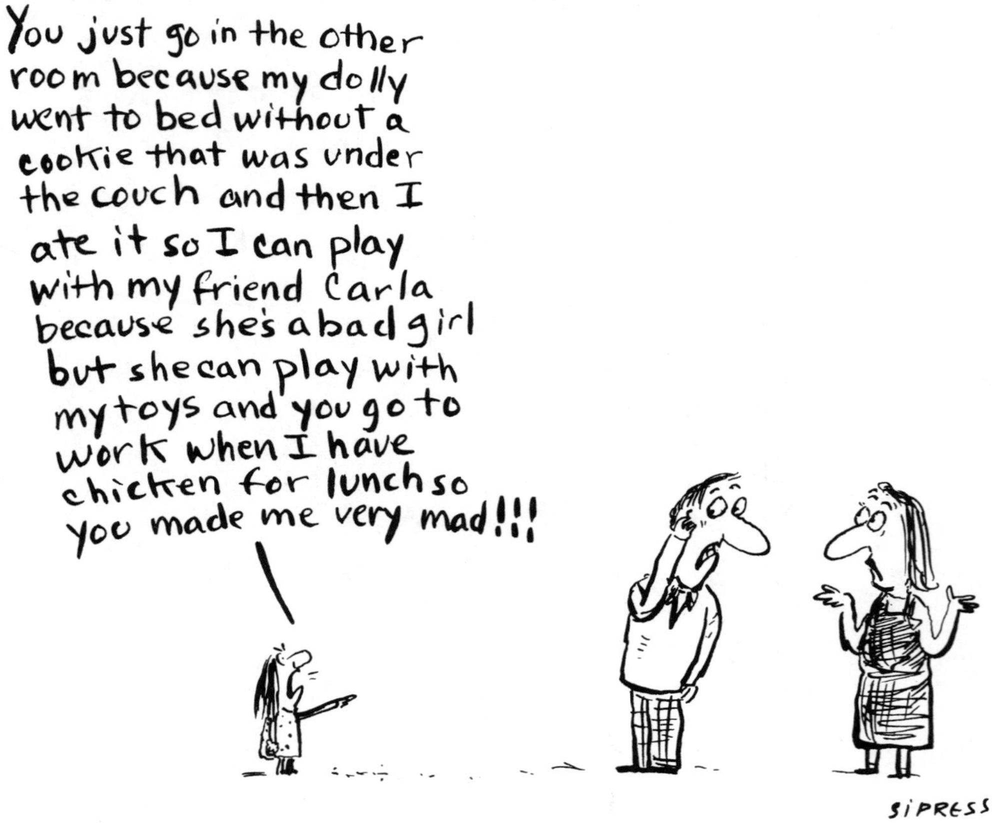
You just go in the other room because my dolly went to bed without a cookie that was under the couch and then I ate it so I can play with my friend Carla because she's a bad girl but she can play with my toys and you go to work when I have chicken for lunch so you made me very mad!!!
SIPRESS

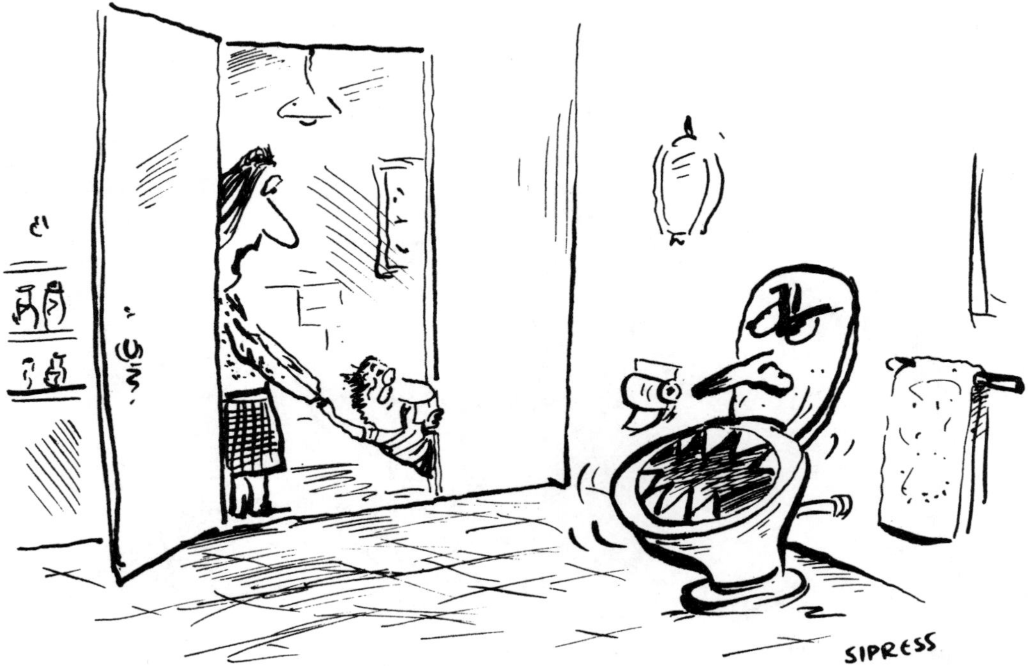
SIPRESS

Please try, Sweetie, there's really nothing to be afraid of!

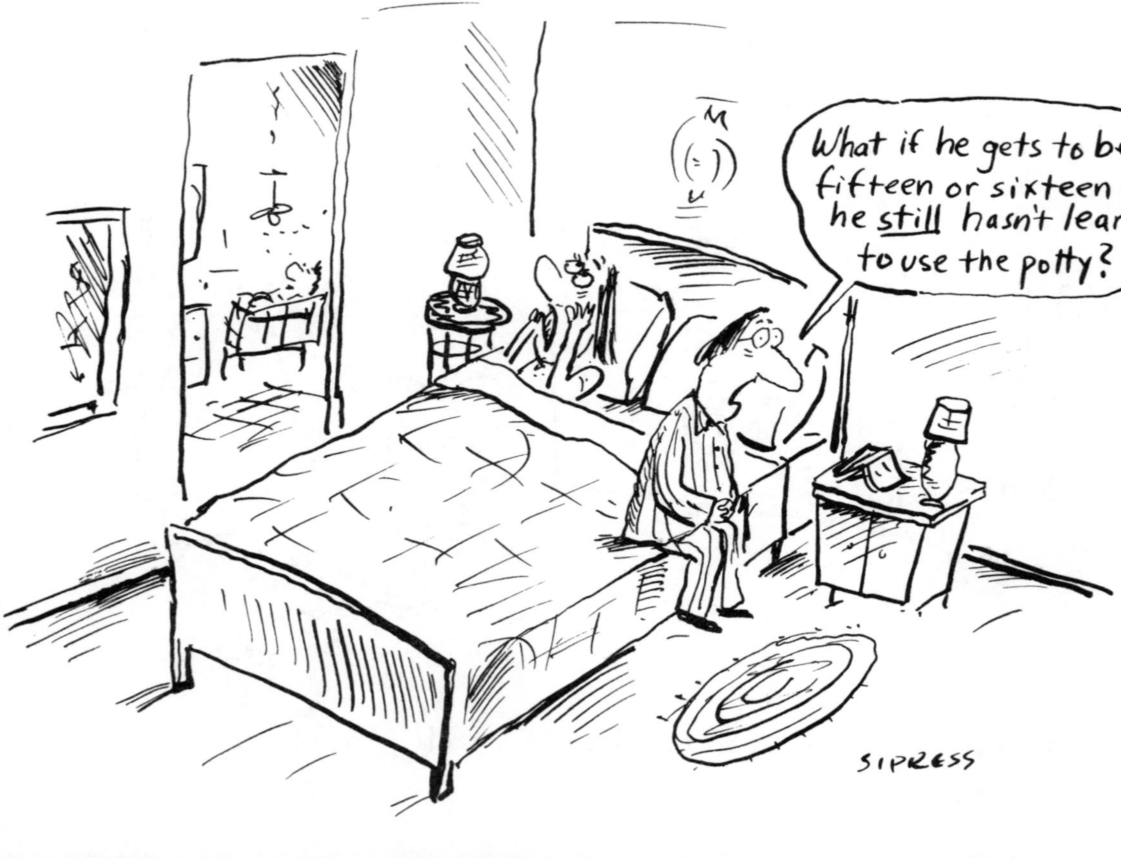
What if he gets to be fifteen or sixteen and he still hasn't learned to use the potty?
SIPRESS

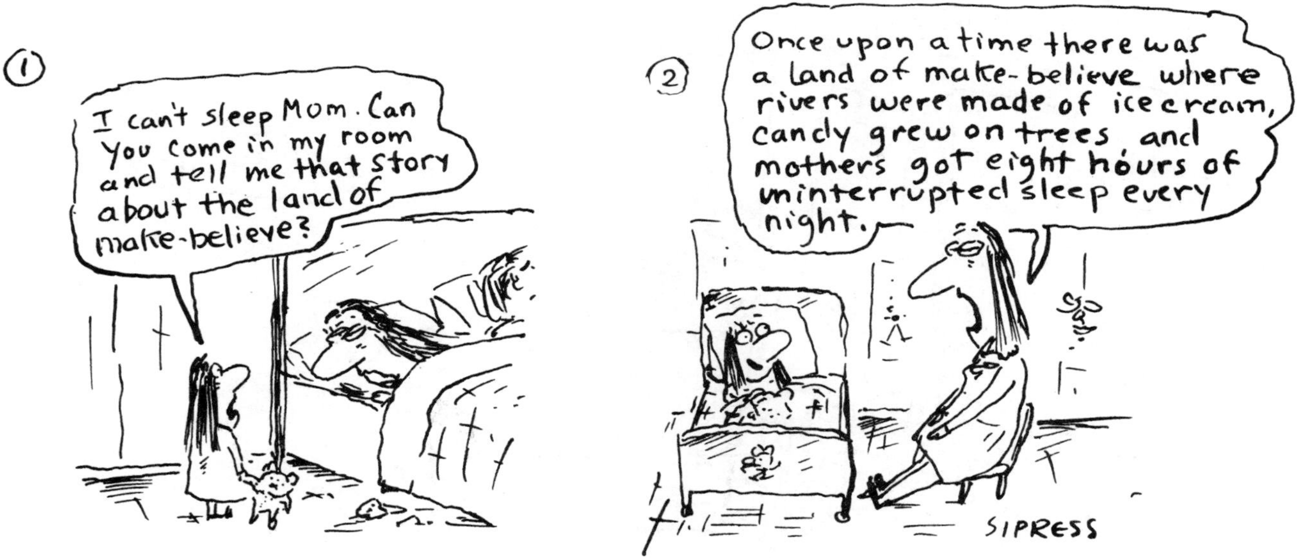
1
I can't sleep Mom. Can you come in my room and tell me that story about the land of make-believe?
2
Once upon a time there was a land of make-believe where rivers were made of ice cream, candy grew on trees and mothers got eight hours of uninterrupted sleep every night.
SIPRESS

HAPPY TIME DAY CARE
Karen, please! Let's go to work! We'll see her later!
SIPRESS

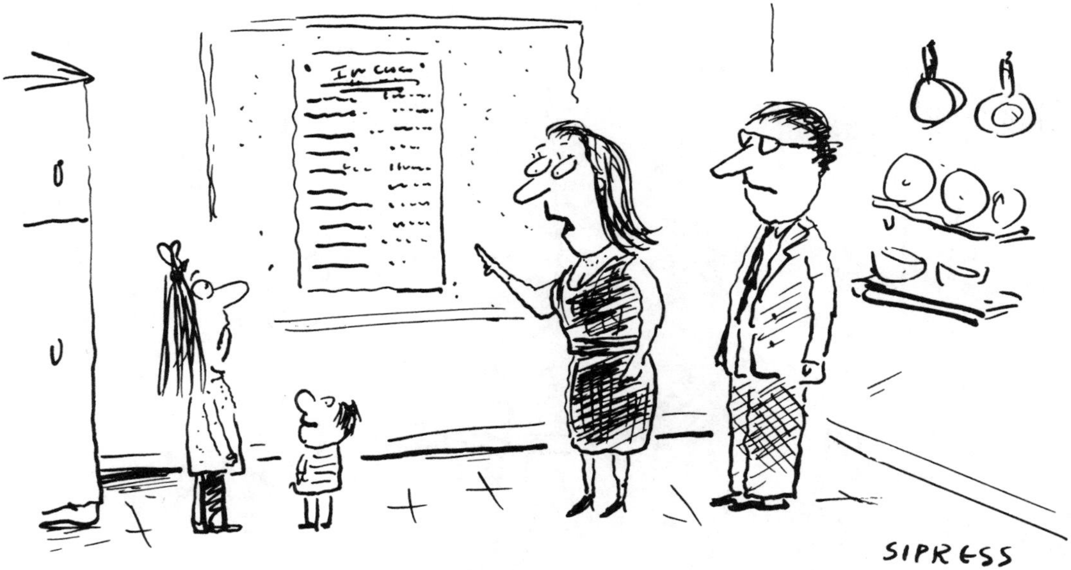
SIPRESS

So, incase of emergency, here are the numbers for the police, the fire department, three hospitals, the F.B.I., the Rescue squad, the Environmental Protection Agency, Civil Defense, the Red Cross, and the Swat Team.

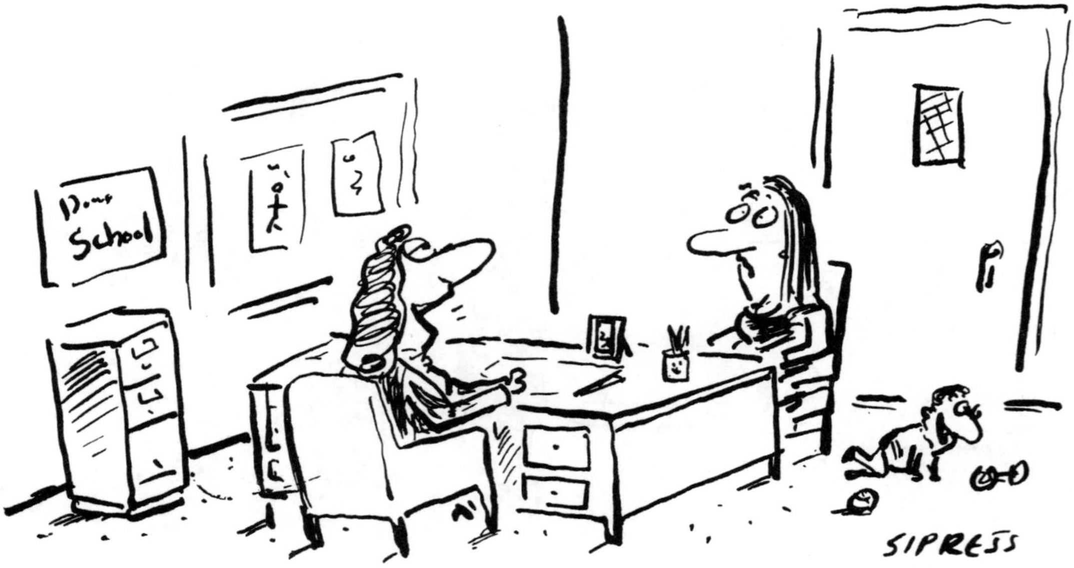
School
SIPRESS

I'm proud to say that graduates of <u>our</u> pre-school have gone on to some of the finest kindergartens in the state!

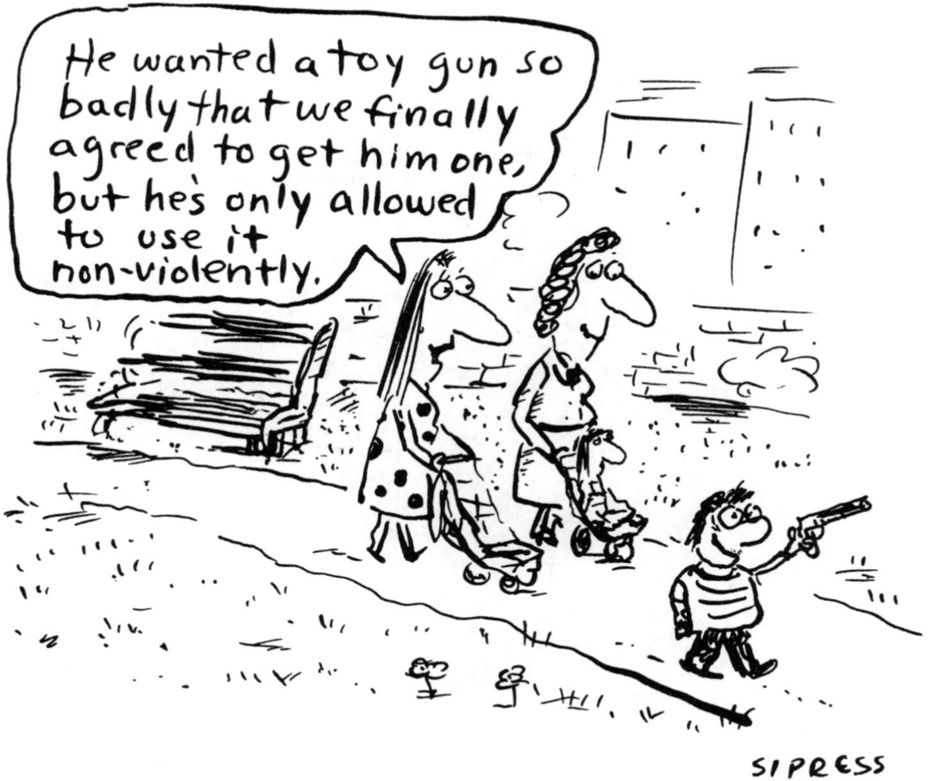
He wanted a toy gun so badly that we finally agreed to get him one, but he's only allowed to use it non-violently.
SIPRESS

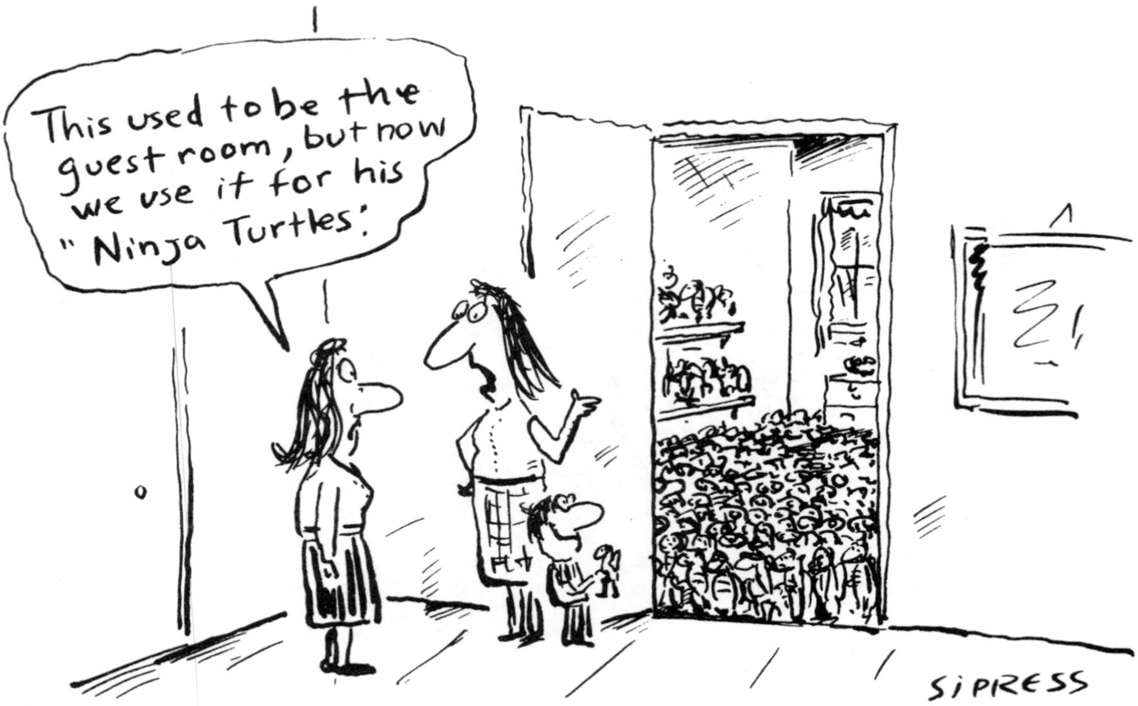
This used to be the guest room, but now we use it for his "Ninja Turtles."
SIPRESS

Now sweetheart, you know it's not very grown up to spill your ice cream all over the couch and it's not nice to leave toys everywhere so that I have to pick them up...
blah blah blah blahty blah blah 'ice cream' blah blah blah blahty blahty blah blah 'toys' blah blah...
SIPRESS

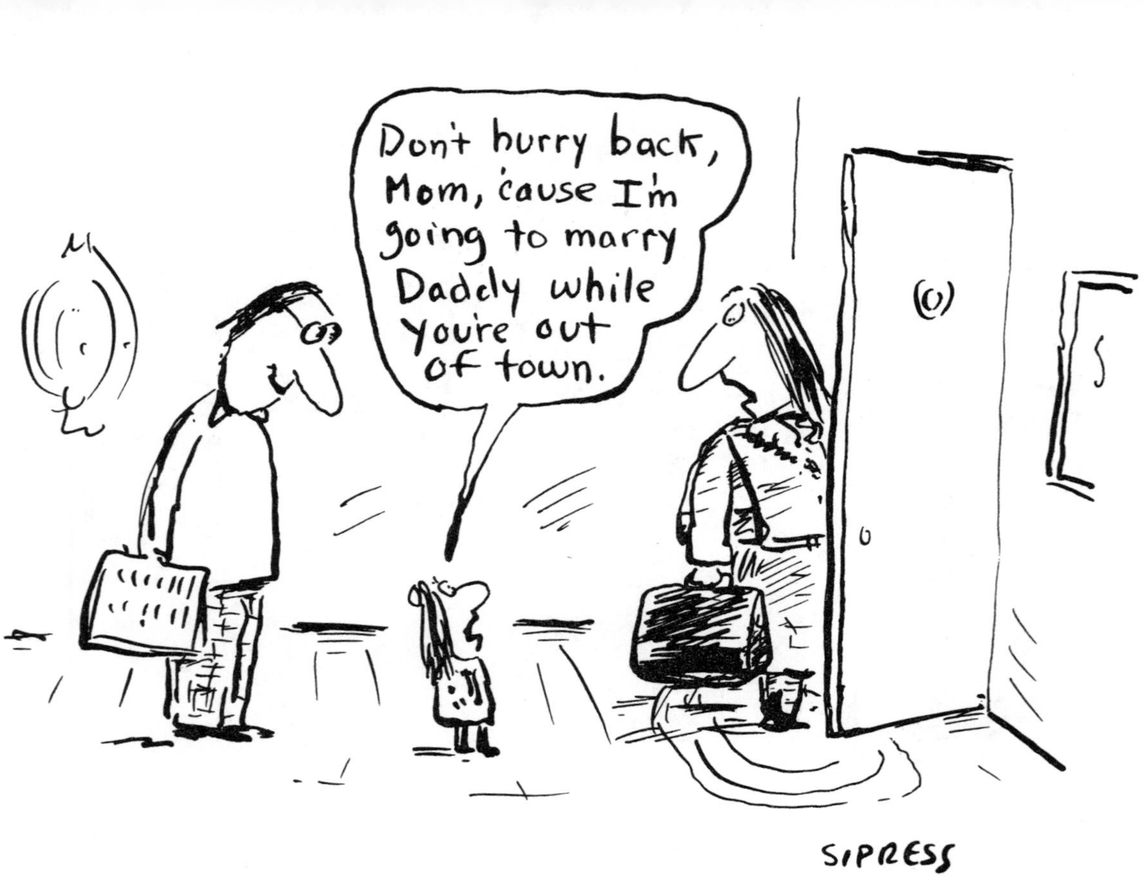
Don't hurry back, Mom, 'cause I'm going to marry Daddy while you're out of town.
SIPRESS

Early Signs of Basic Differences between the Sexes:

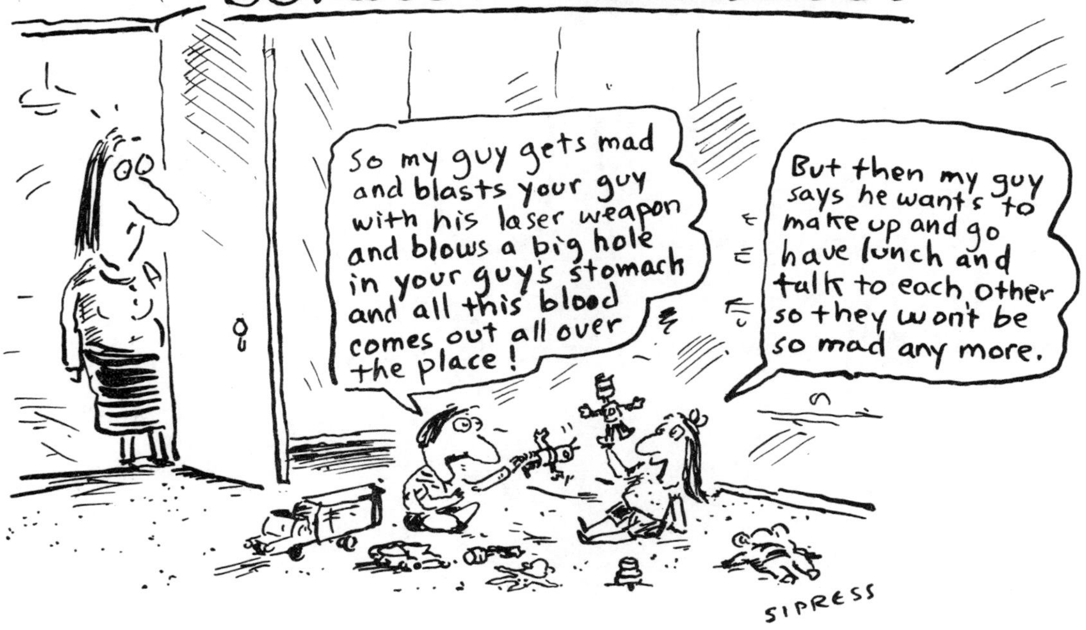
So my guy gets mad and blasts your guy with his laser weapon and blows a big hole in your guy's stomach and all this blood comes out all over the place!
But then my guy says he want's to make up and go have lunch and talk to each other so they won't be so mad any more.
SIPRESS

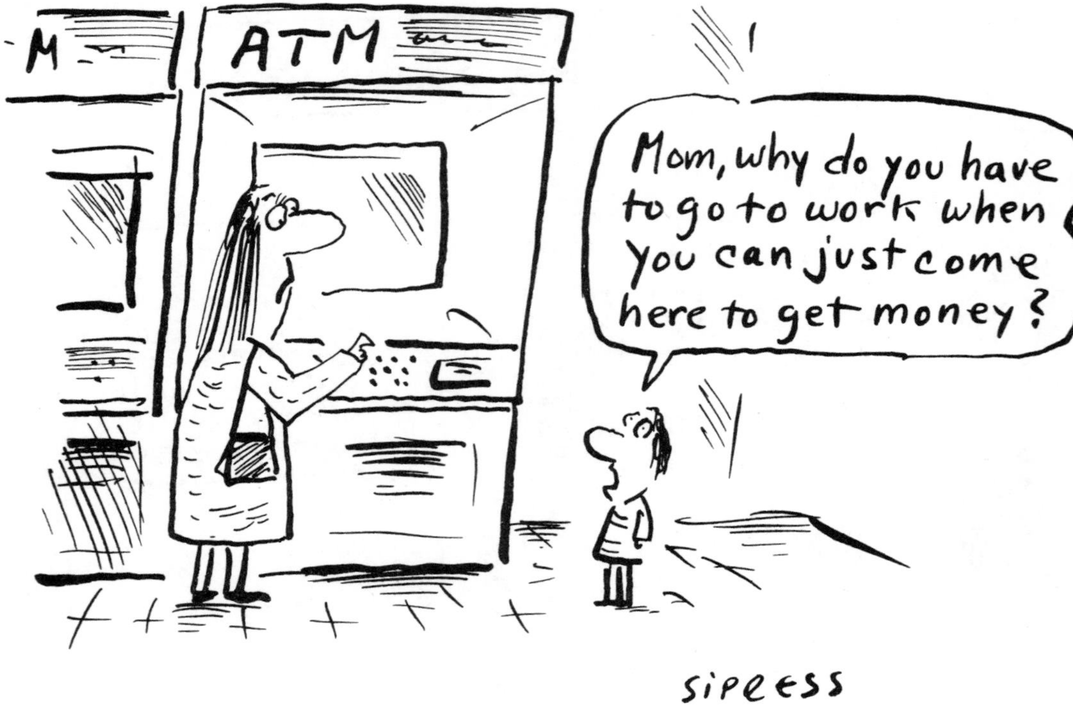
M
ATM
Mom, why do you have to go to work when you can just come here to get money?
sipress

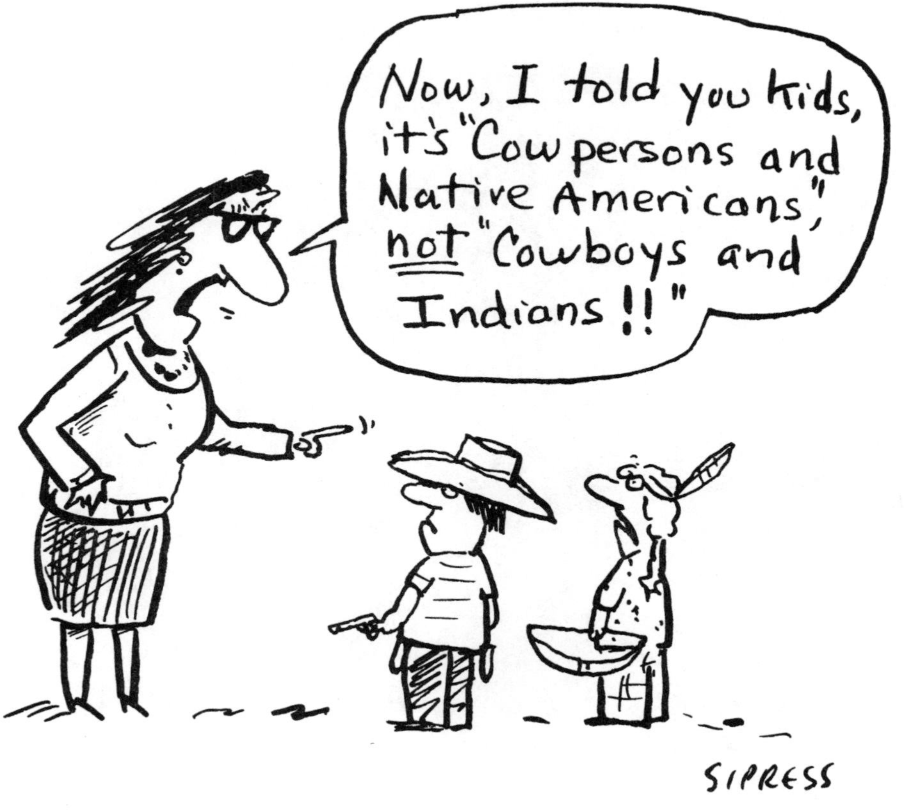
Now, I told you kids, it's "Cowpersons and Native Americans," not "Cowboys and Indians!!"
SIPRESS

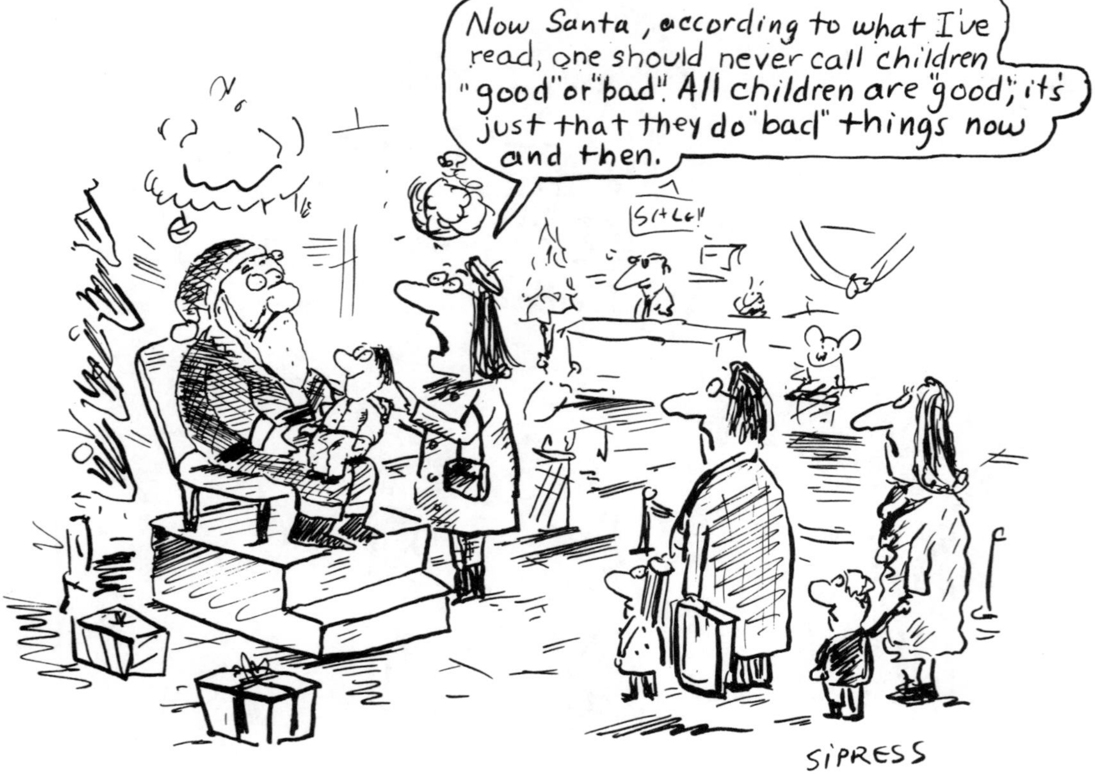
Now Santa, according to what I've read, one should never call children "good" or "bad". All children are "good"; it's just that they do "bad" things now and then.
SIPRESS

Moms Through the Ages

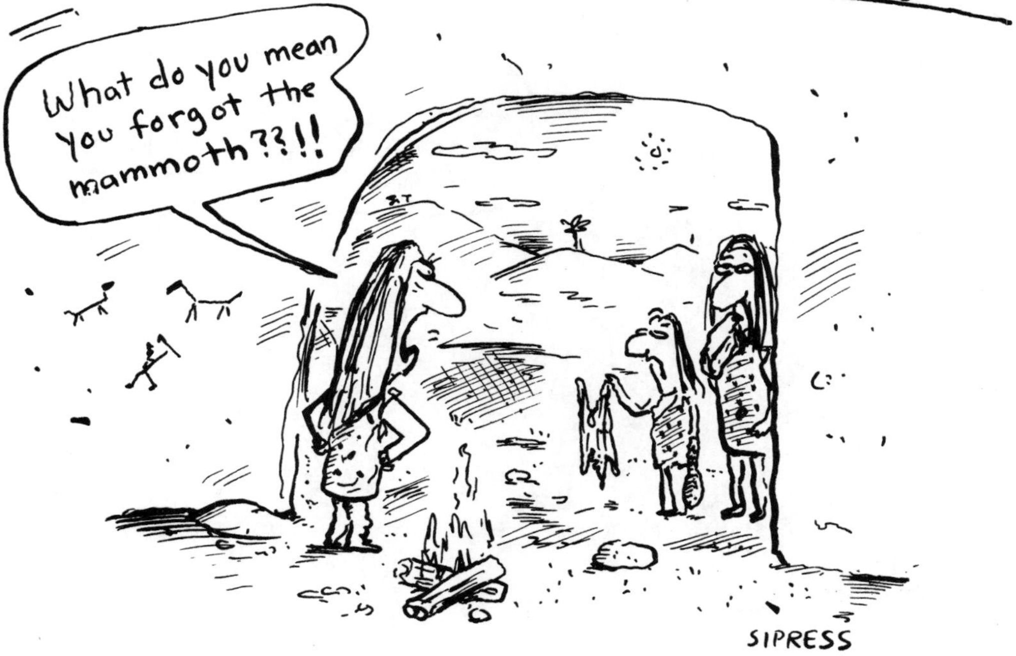
What do you mean you forgot the mammoth??!!
SIPRESS

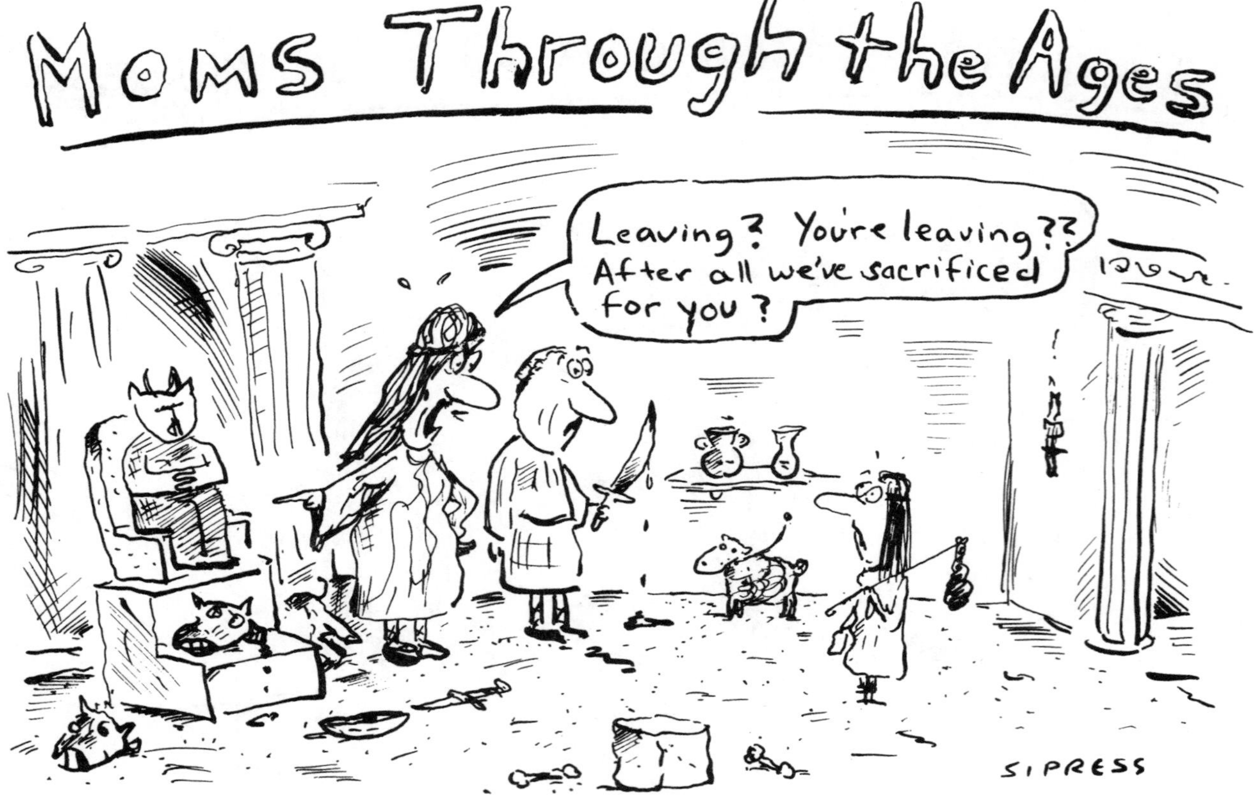
Moms Through the Ages
Leaving? You're leaving?? After all we've sacrificed for you?
SIPRESS

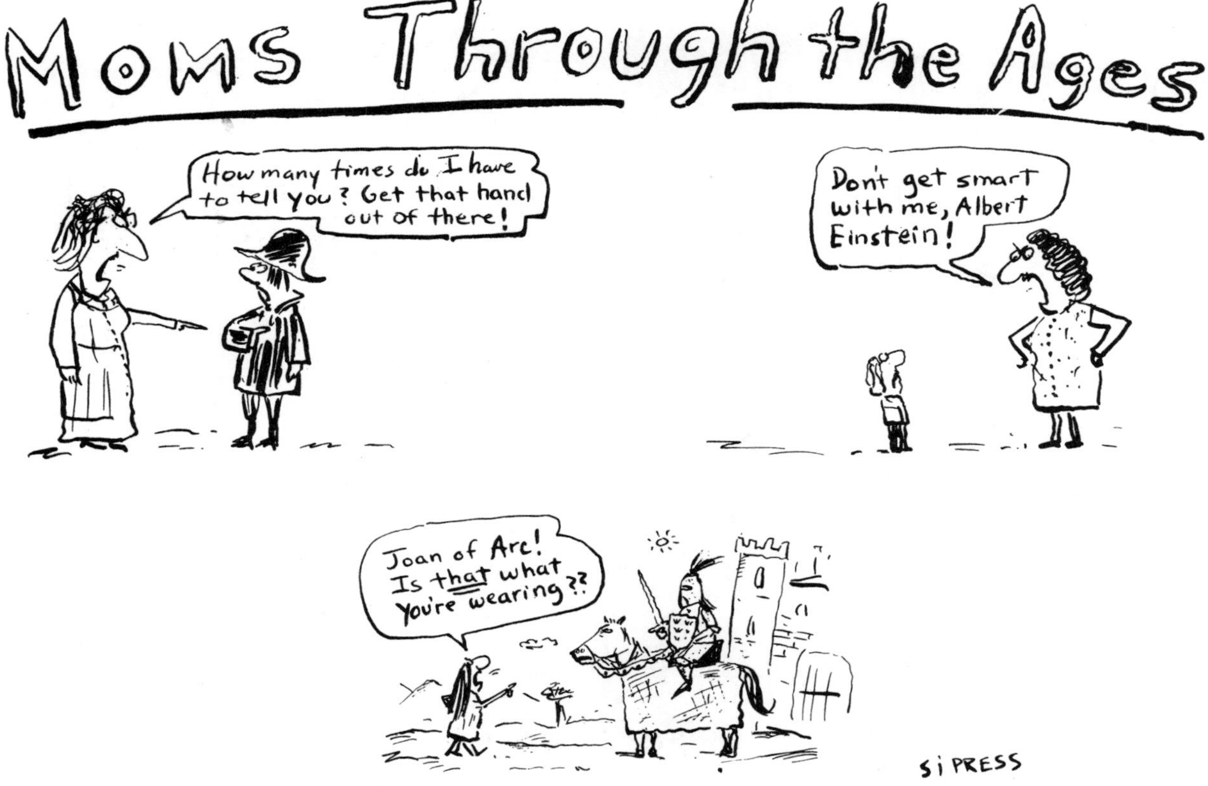
Moms Through the Ages
How many times do I have to tell you? Get that hand out of there!
Don't get smart with me, Albert Einstein!
Joan of Arc! Is that what you're wearing??
si PRESS

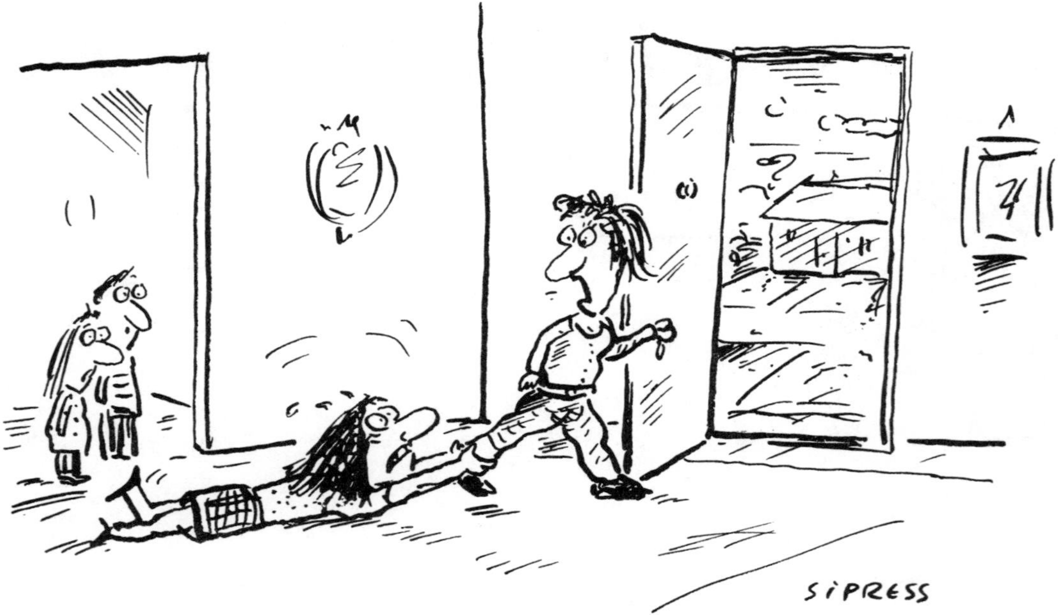
SIPRESS

Please, Mrs. Martin, I have to go to college! I can't baby-sit forever!

MY ELEMENTARY SCHOOL COSTS EIGHT THOUSAND DOLLARS A YEAR!!
OH, YEAH? WELL, MINE COSTS NINE THOUSAND A YEAR!
SIPRESS

Why mothers are constantly sick for years on end.

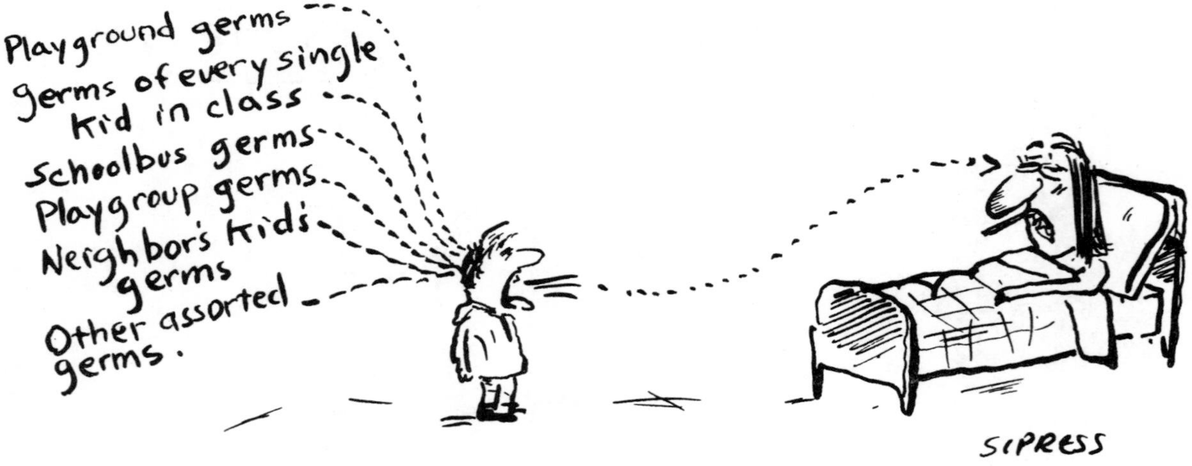

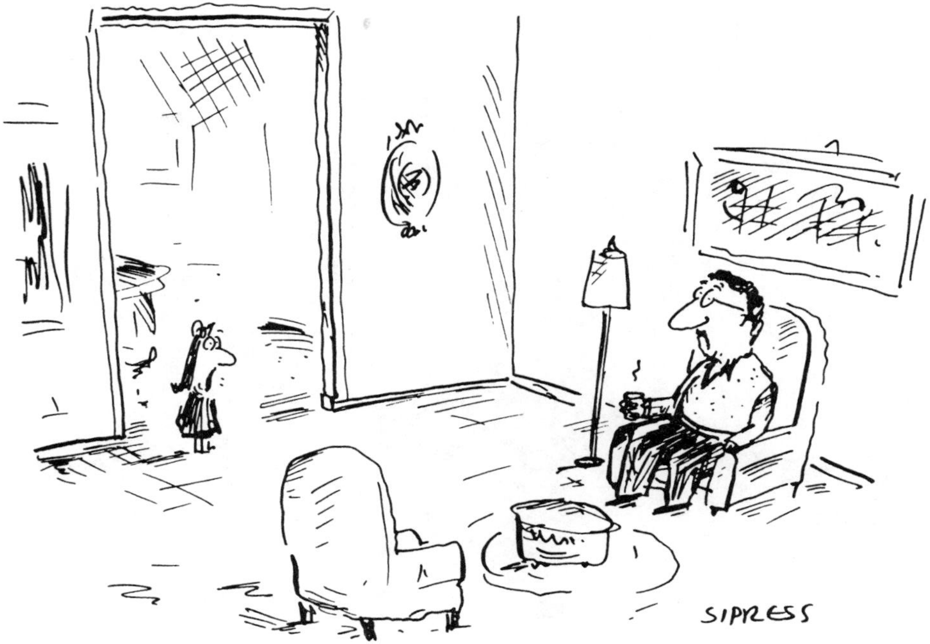
SIPRESS

Mommy says to tell you to run me a bath, fix me a snack, and explain to me where babies come from.

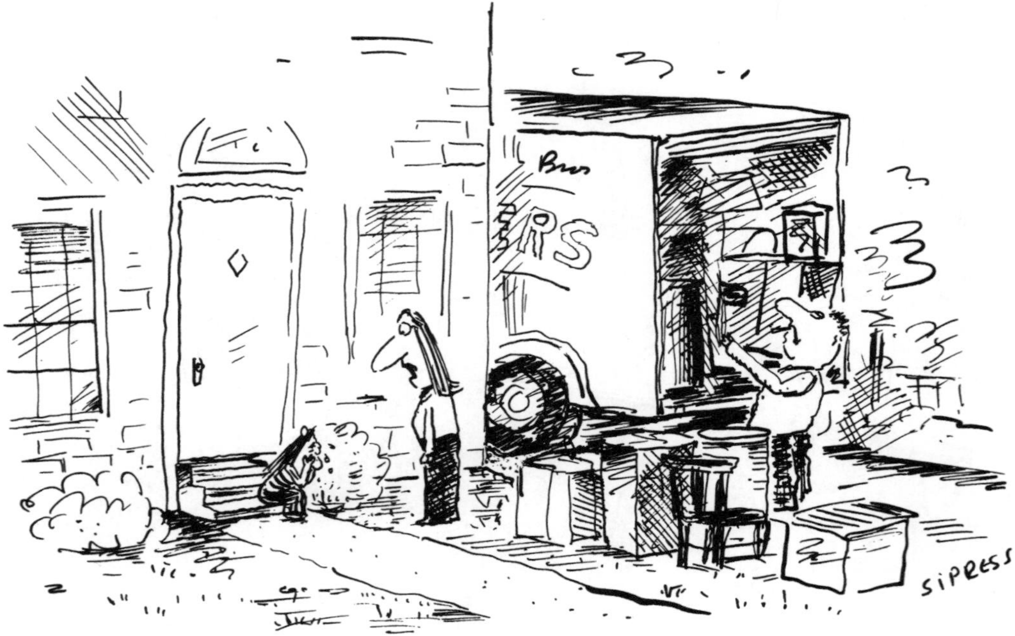
Bros
RS
SIPRESS

Sweetheart, we put all your toys and furniture and stuff in the truck, but there's no way we can move the room itself.

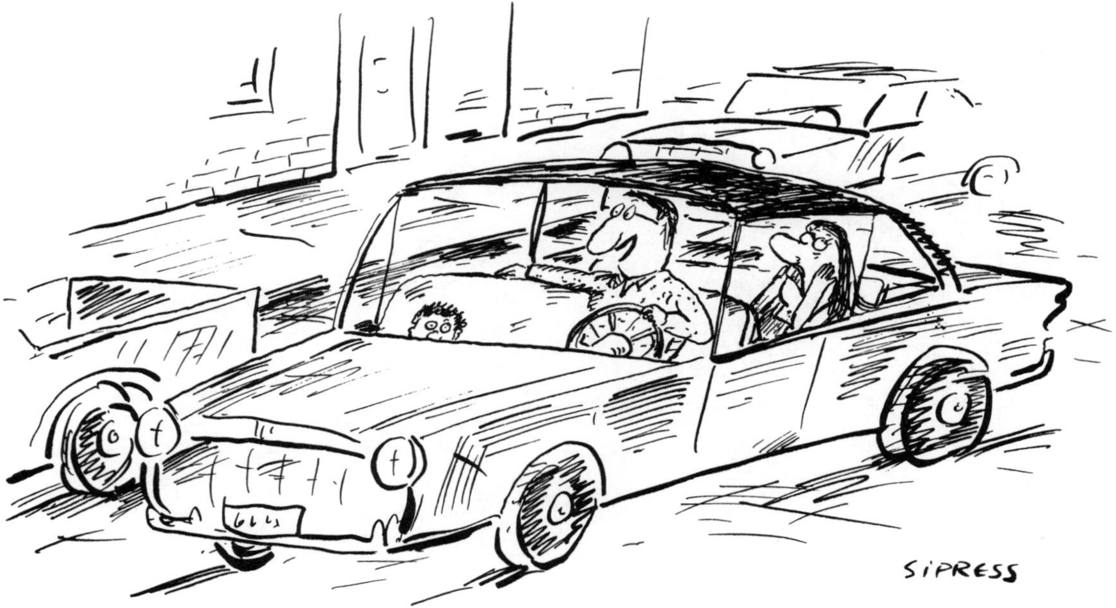
SIPRESS

Your Dad's about to parallel park, son. Just watch, you may learn something!

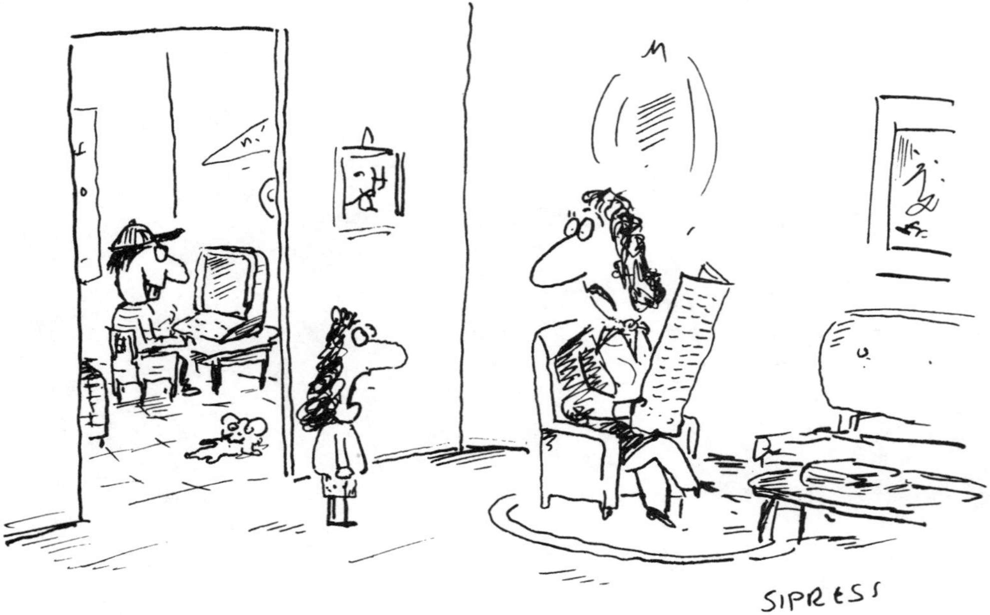
SIPRESS

Mom! Will you please tell Michael to quit stealing Defense Department secrets with <u>my</u> computer??!!

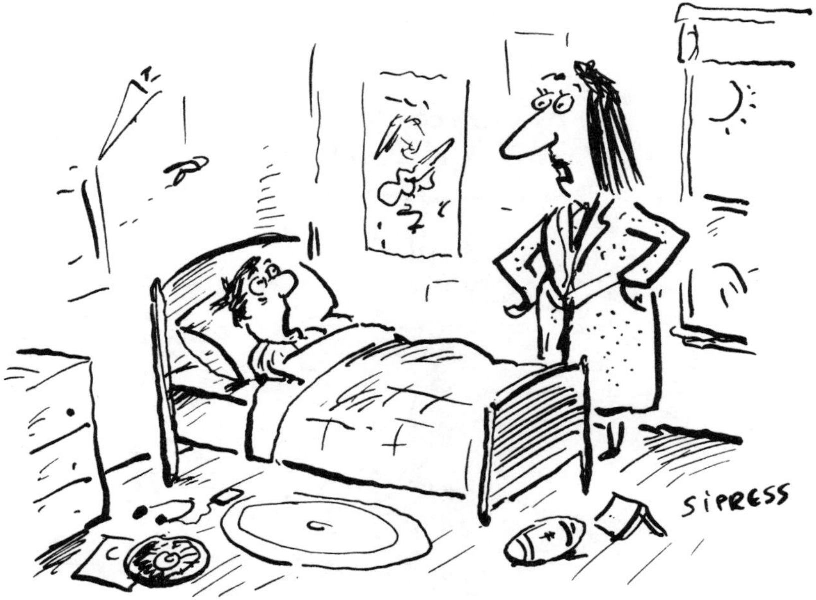
SIPRESS

Well, nothing hurts exactly, it's more a kind of existential angst.

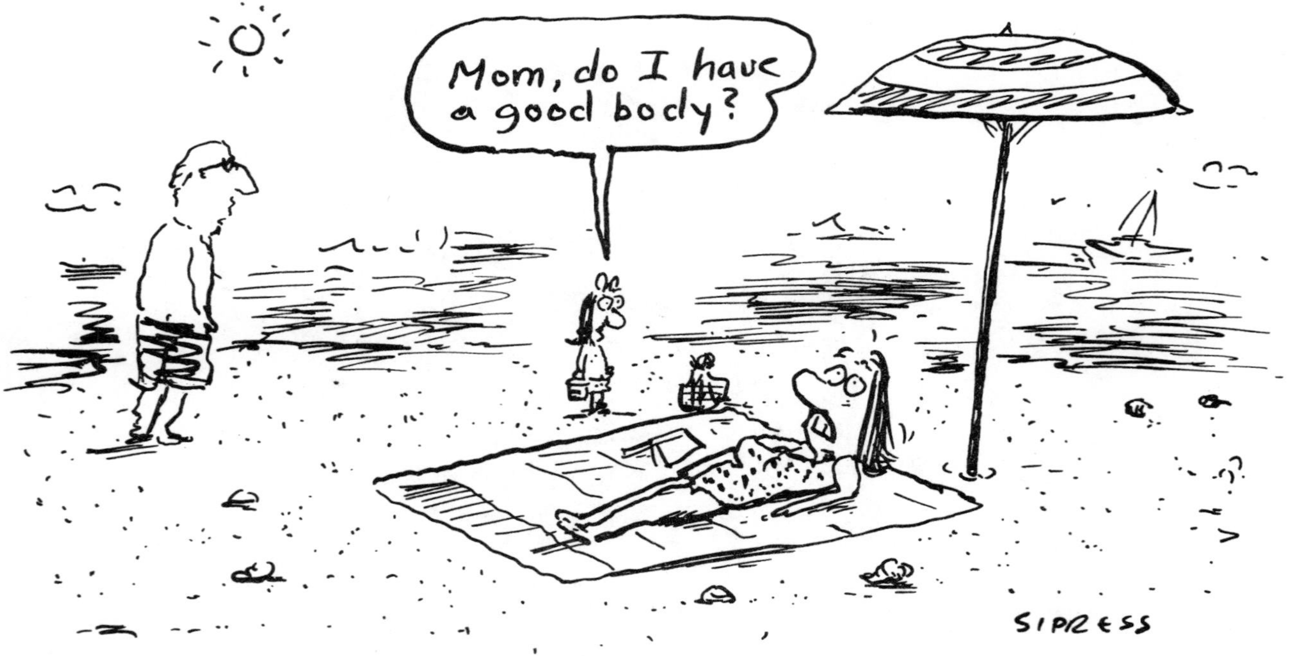
Mom, do I have a good body?
SIPRESS

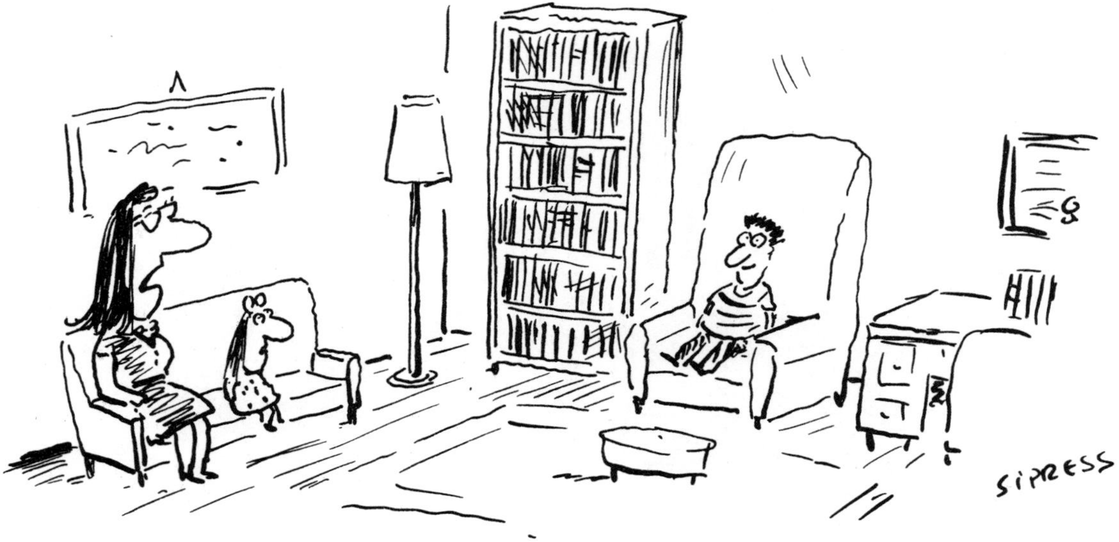
SIPRESS

I guess when I was told you were a "child psychologist" I took it to mean something different.

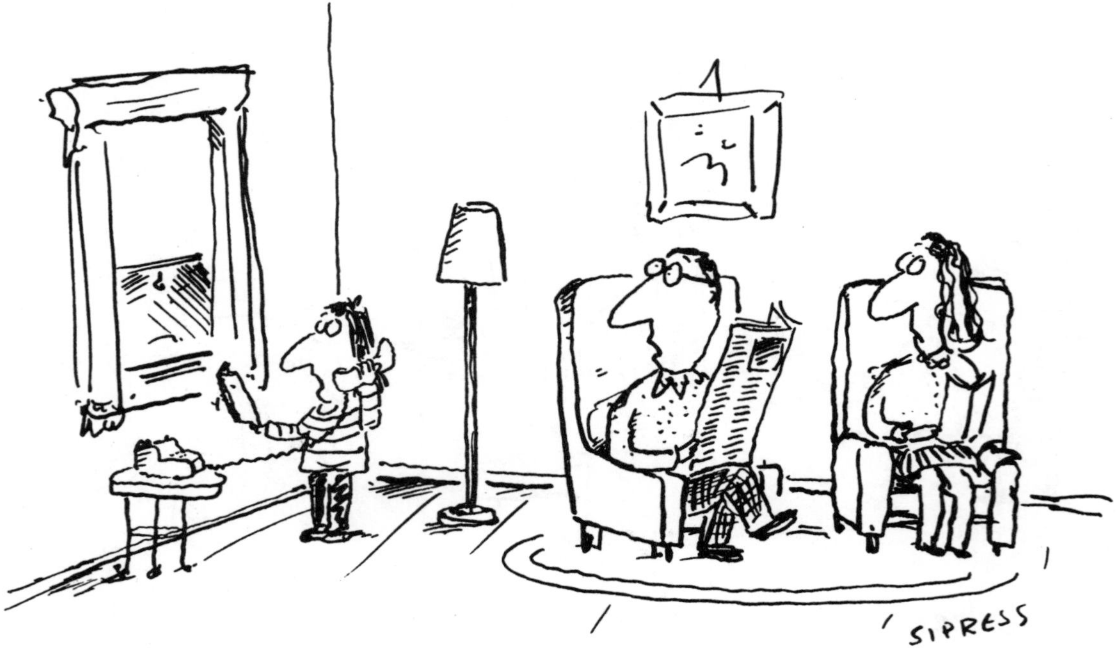
SIPRESS

I'm afraid I don't have a free play-date this week. But let's do milk and cookies sometime.

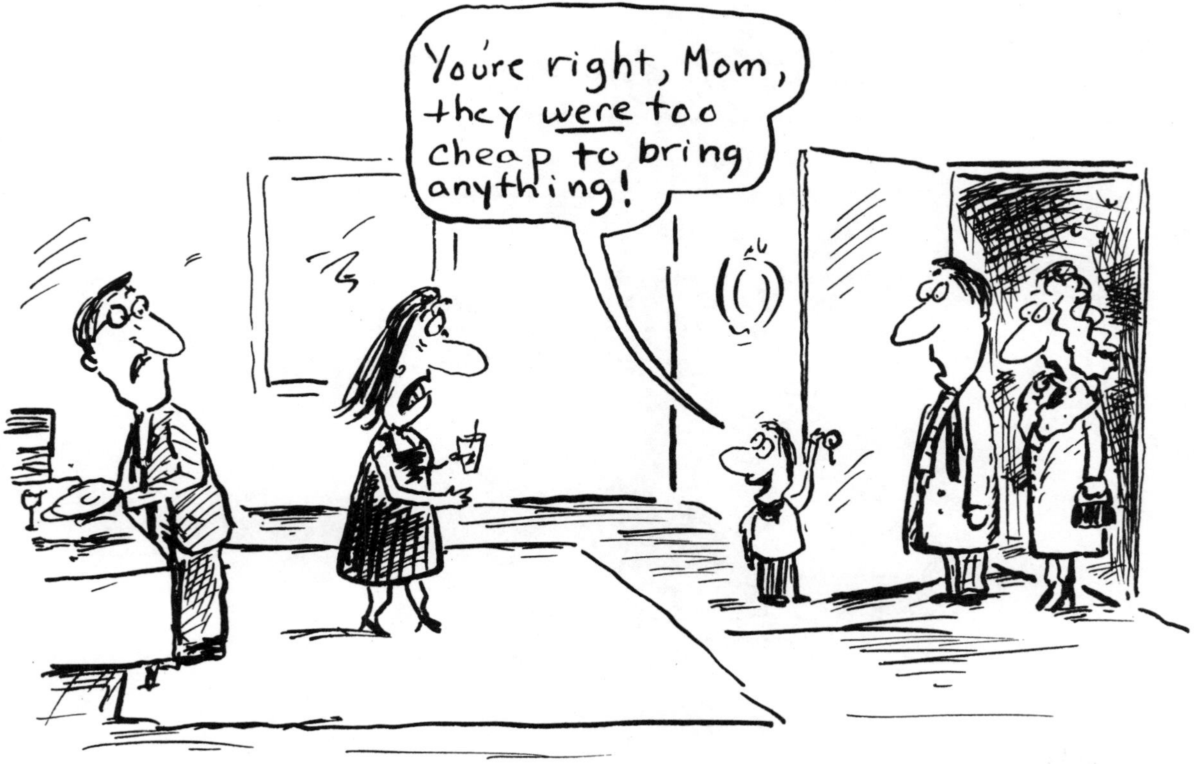
You're right, Mom, they were too cheap to bring anything!
SIPRESS

ONE OF LIFE'S GREAT MYSTERIES:

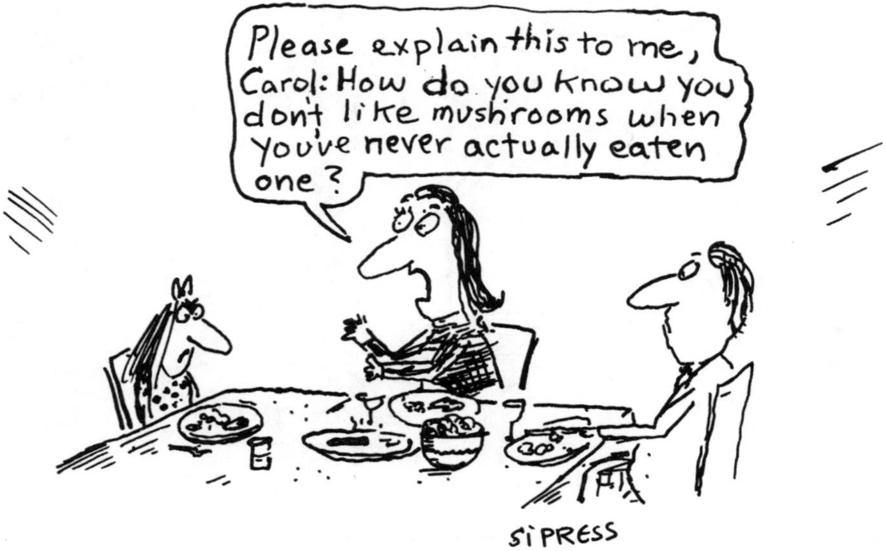
Please explain this to me, Carol: How do you know you don't like mushrooms when you've never actually eaten one?
SIPRESS

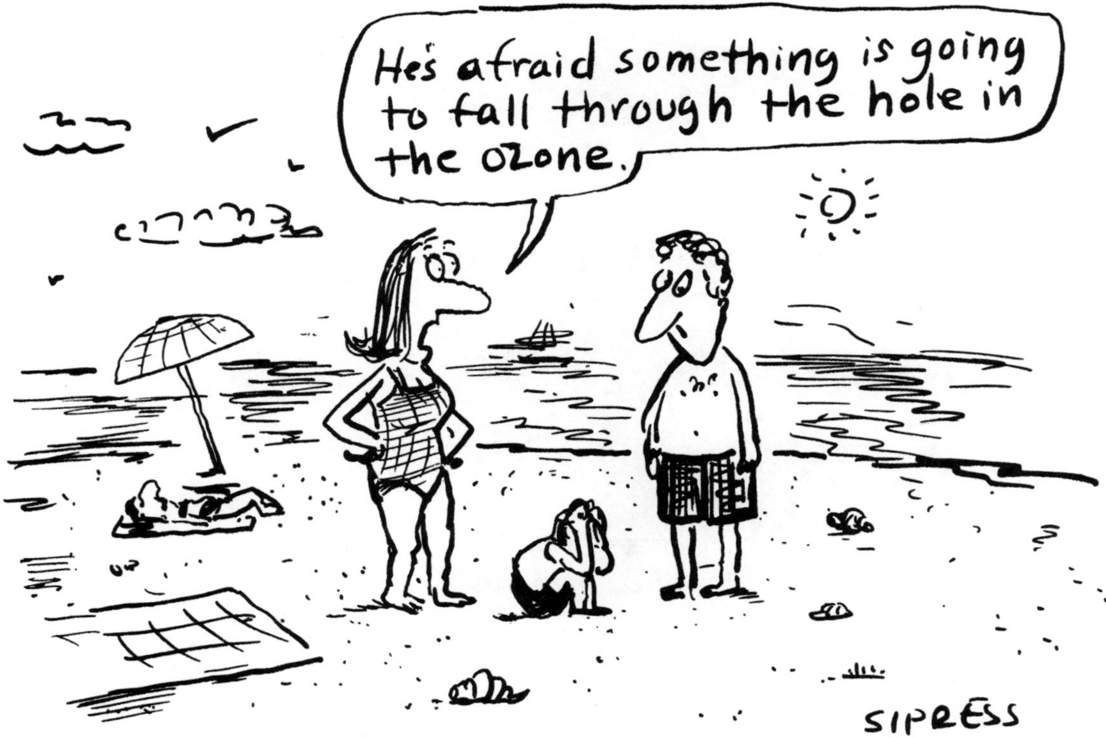
He's afraid something is going to fall through the hole in the ozone.
SIPRESS

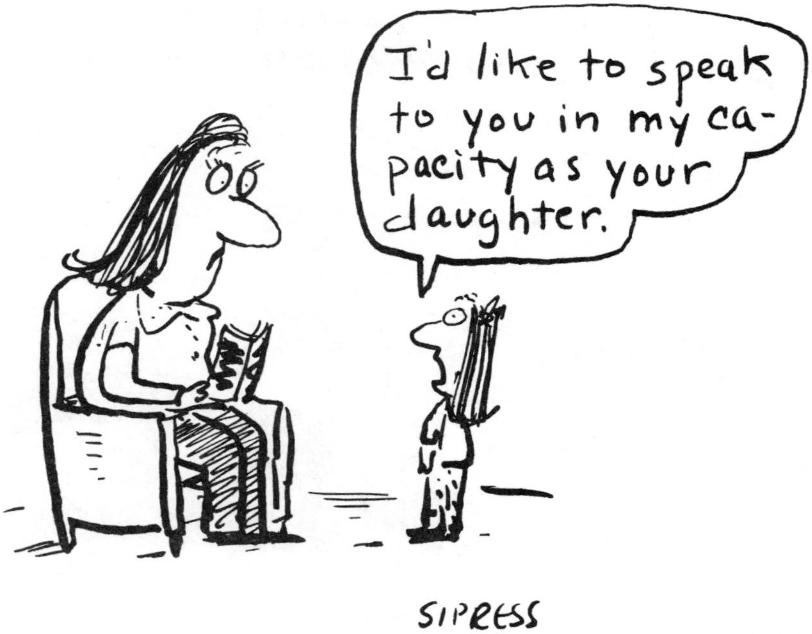
I'd like to speak to you in my capacity as your daughter.
SIPRESS

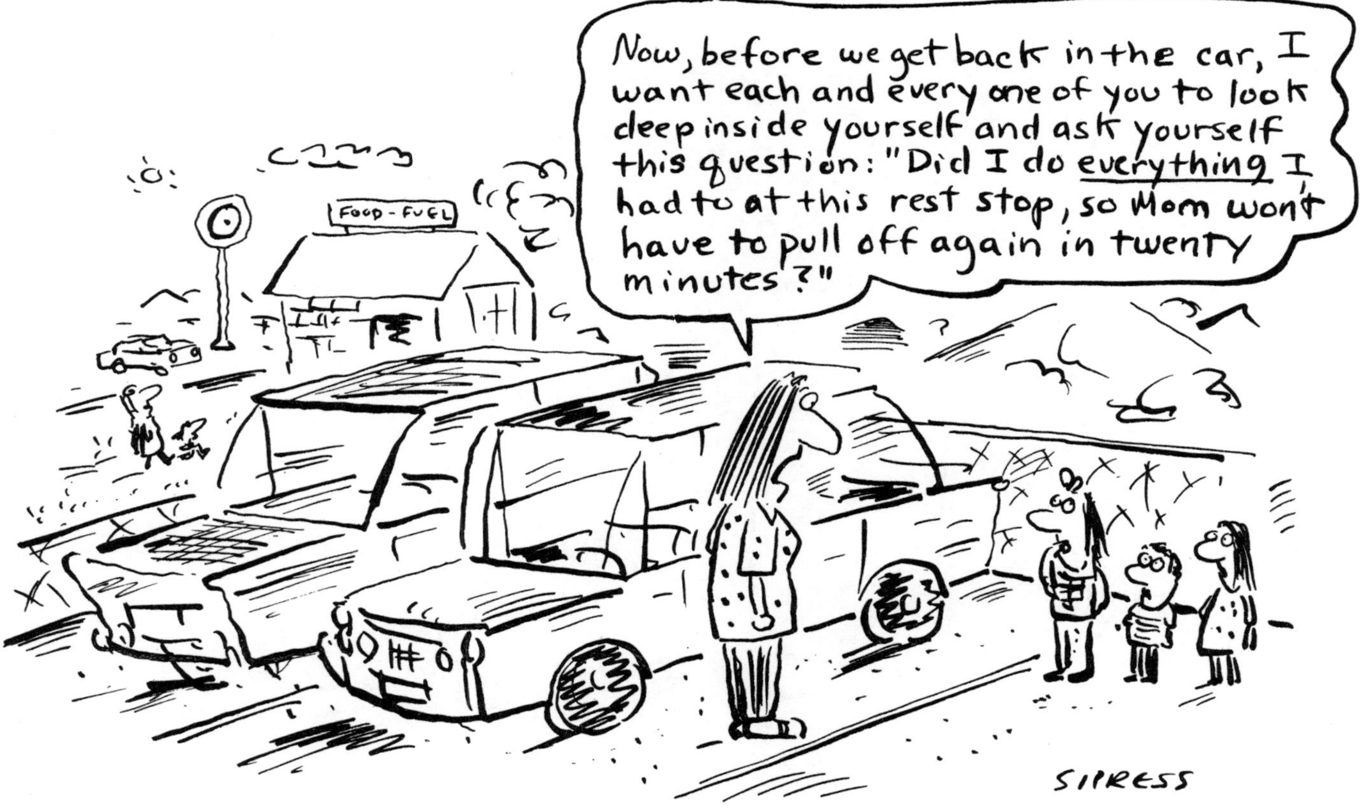
Now, before we get back in the car, I want each and every one of you to look deep inside yourself and ask yourself this question: "Did I do everything I had to at this rest stop, so Mom won't have to pull off again in twenty minutes?"
FOOD - FUEL
SIPRESS

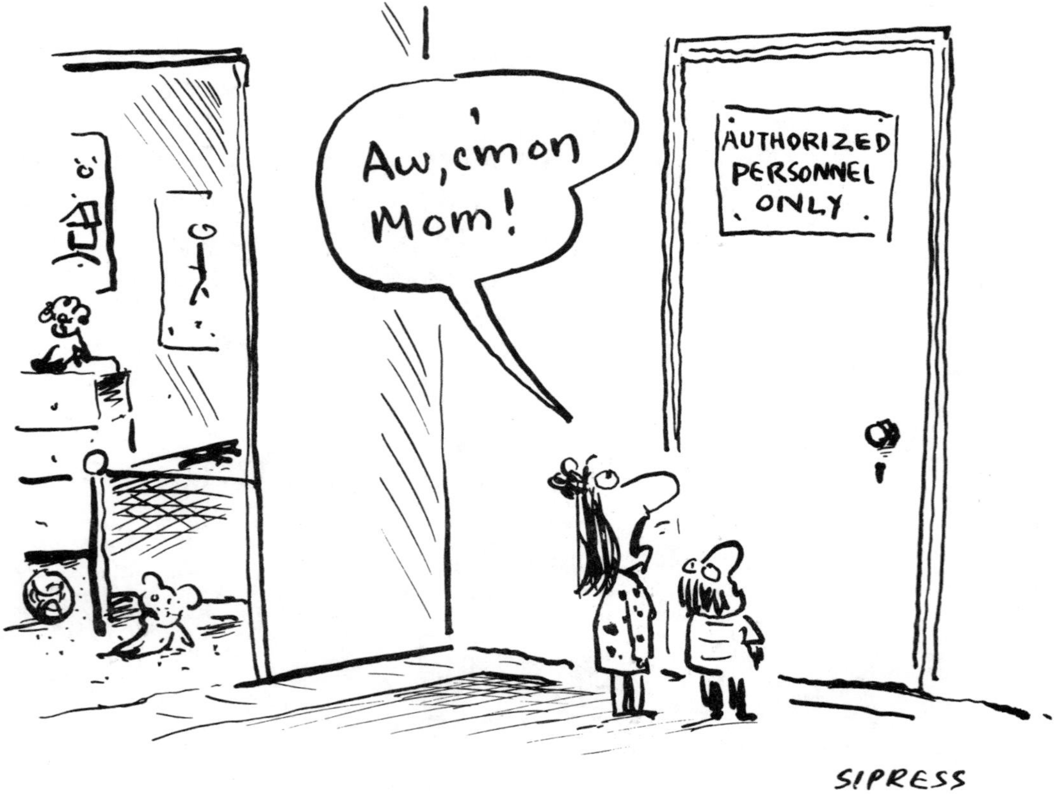
Aw, c'mon Mom!
AUTHORIZED PERSONNEL ONLY
SIPRESS

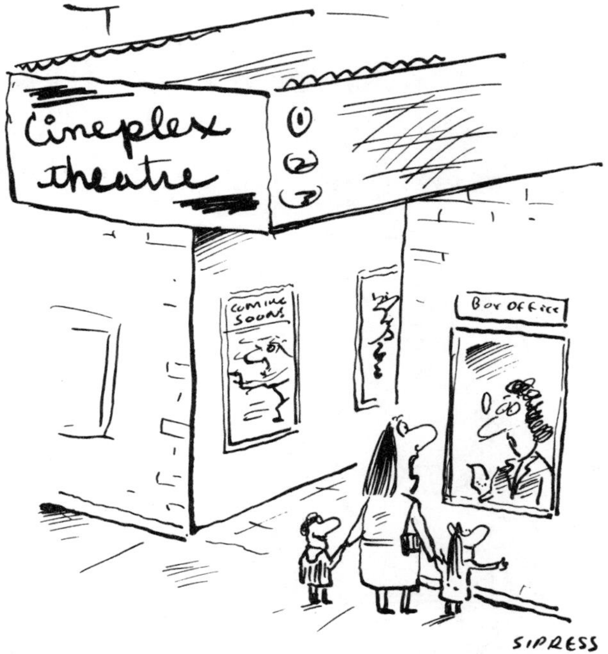
Cineplex theatre
(1)
(2)
(3)
COMING SOON
Box Office
SIPRESS

Do you have any movies featuring obedient, well-behaved children, and kind, understanding parents?

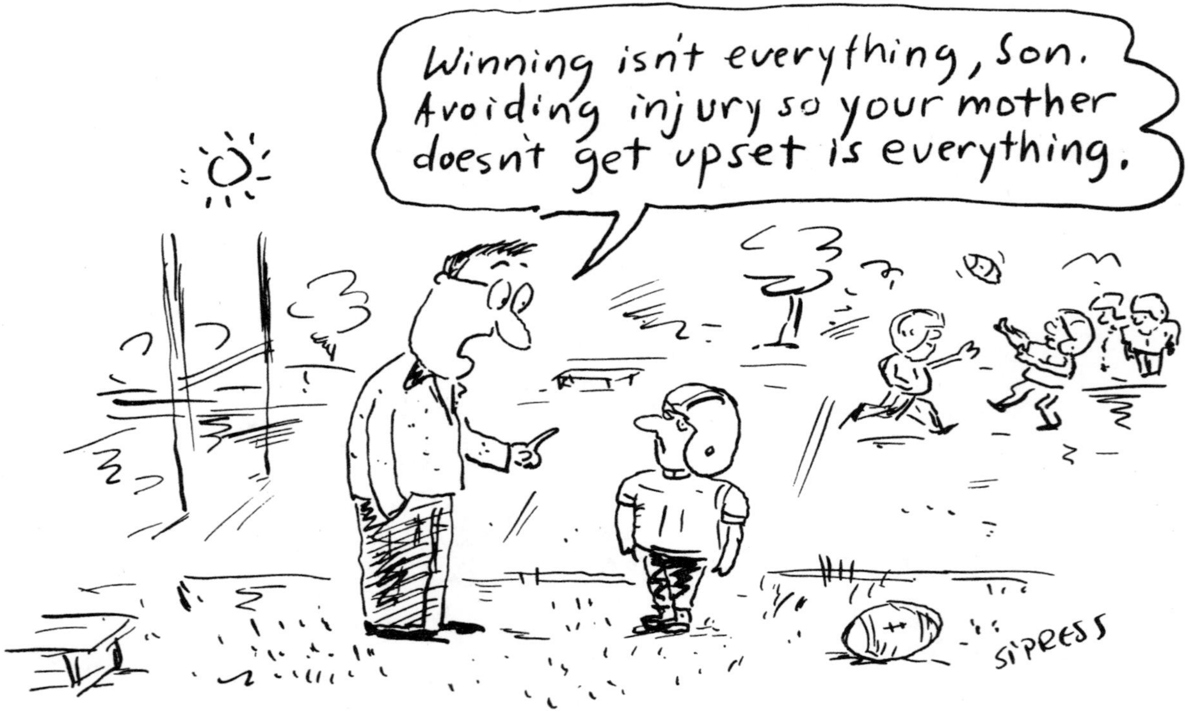
Winning isn't everything, Son. Avoiding injury so your mother doesn't get upset is everything.
SIPRESS

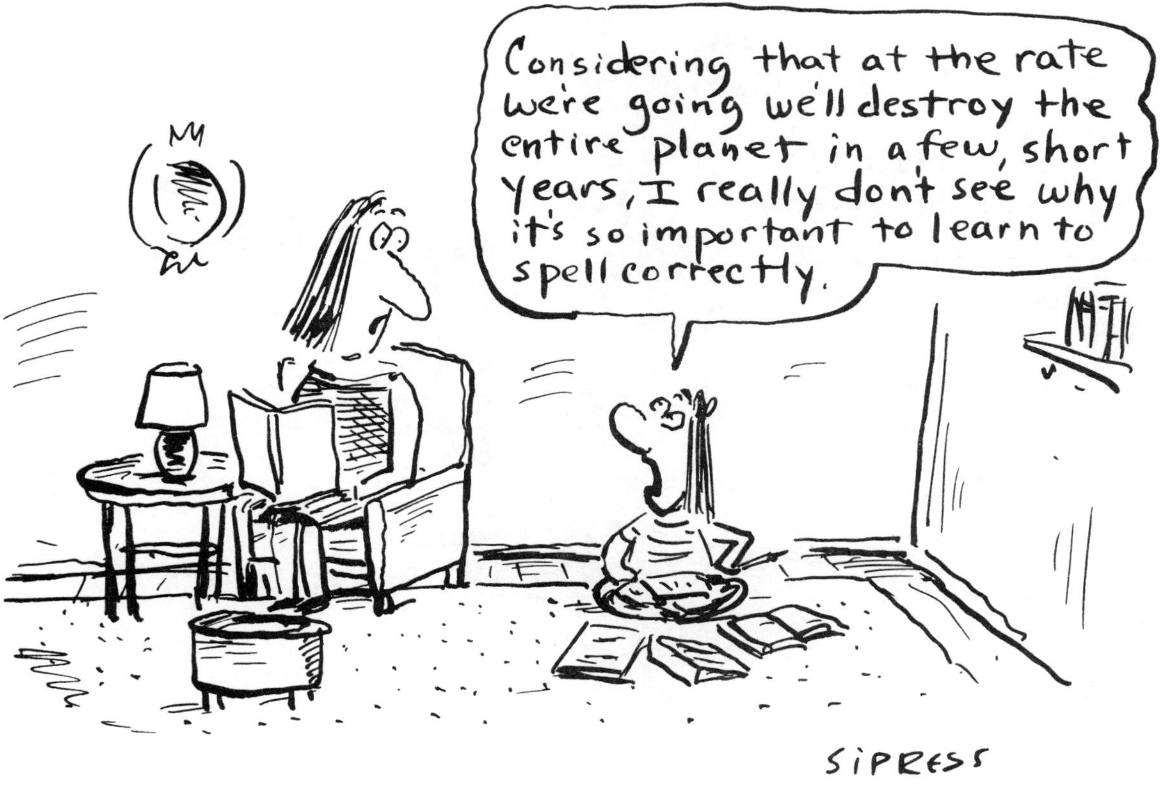
Considering that at the rate we're going we'll destroy the entire planet in a few, short years, I really don't see why it's so important to learn to spell correctly.
SIPRESS

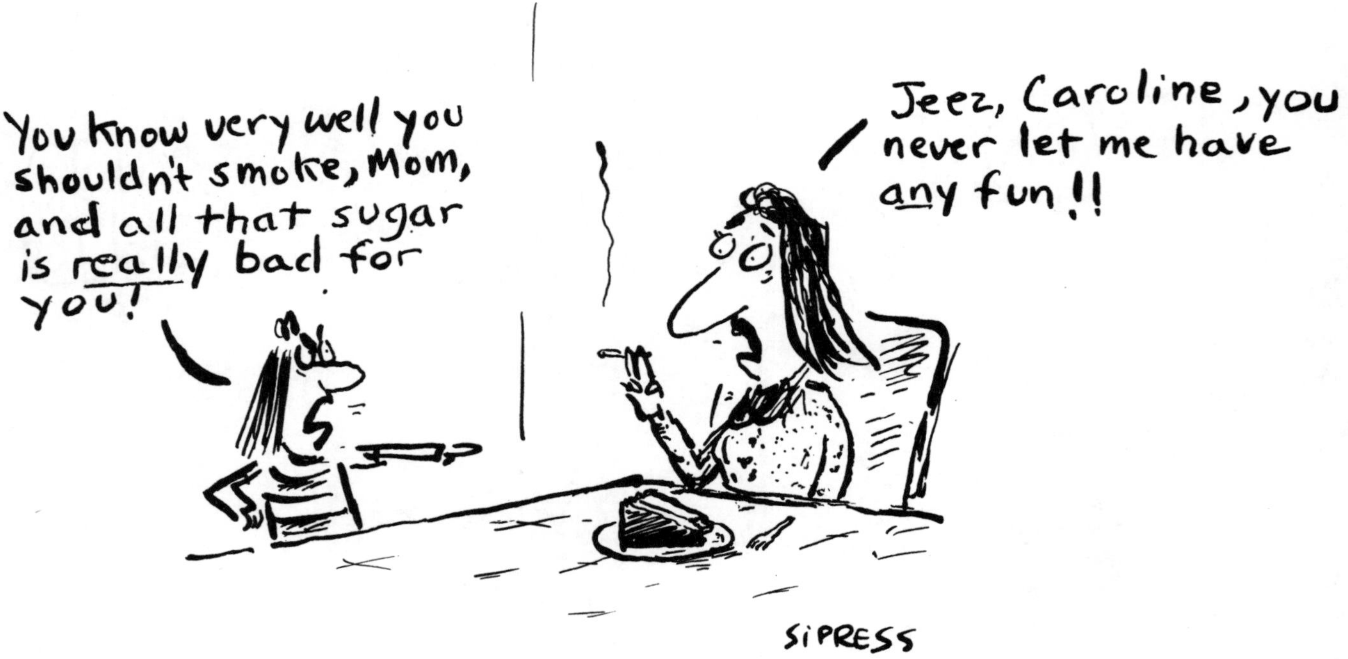
You know very well you shouldn't smoke, Mom, and all that sugar is really bad for you!
Jeez, Caroline, you never let me have any fun!!
SIPRESS

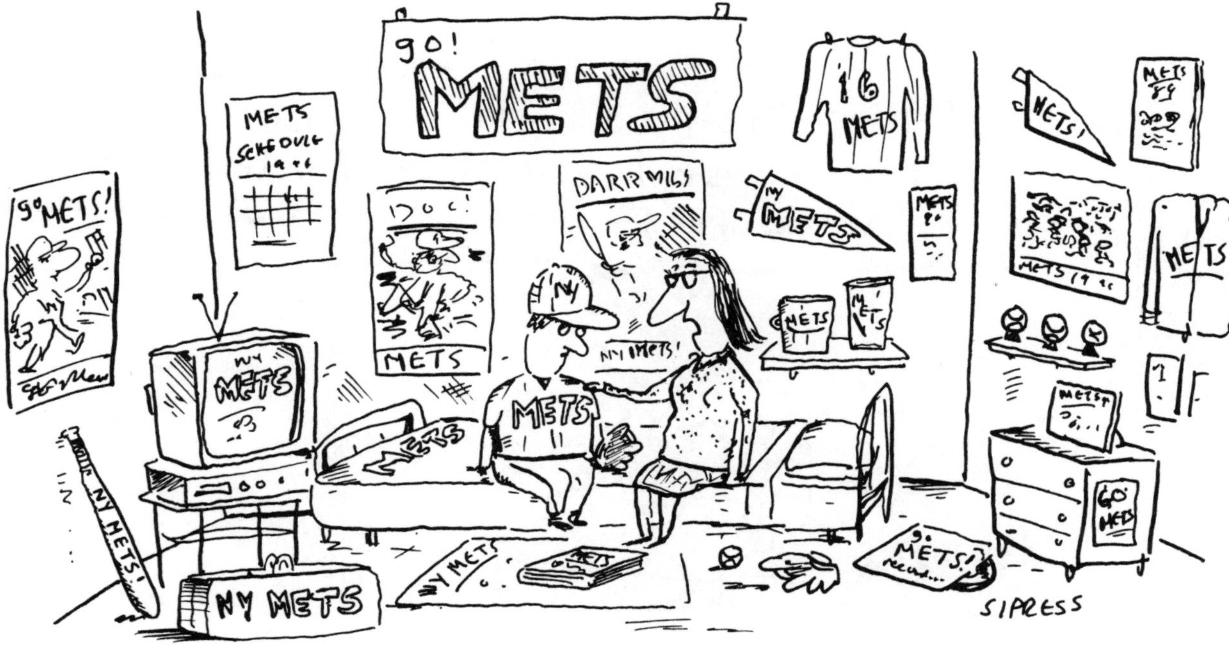
go! METS
METS SCHEDULE
go METS!
NY METS
METS
16 METS
DARR MILLS
NY METS
go METS!
SIPRESS

Honey, are you familiar with the word "obsession?"

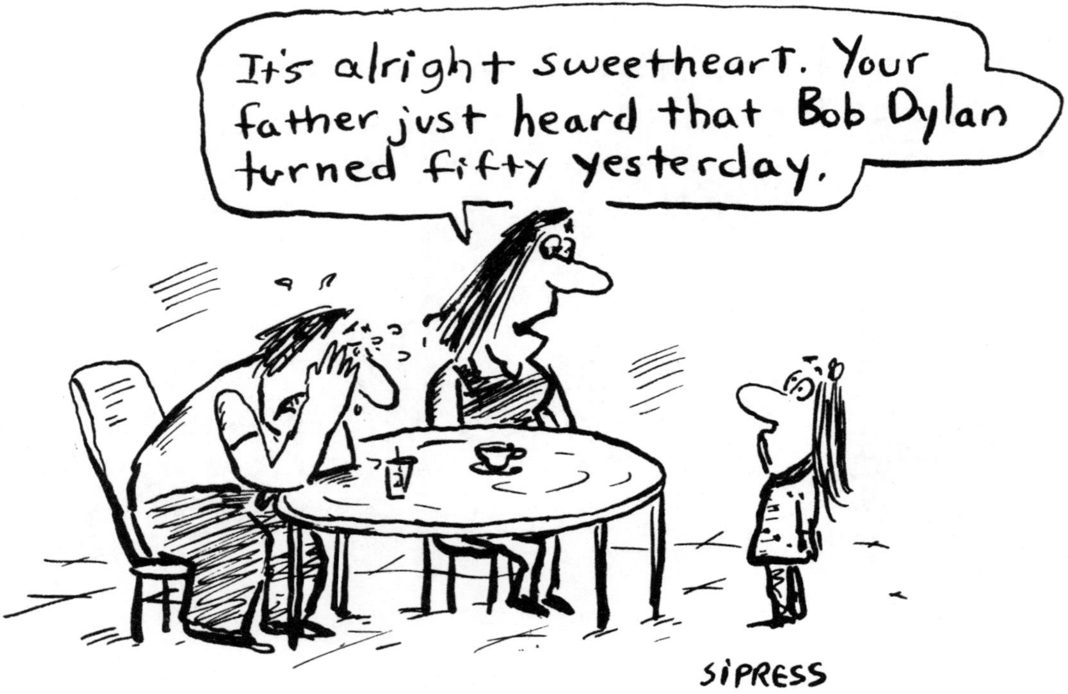
It's alright sweetheart. Your father just heard that Bob Dylan turned fifty yesterday.
SIPRESS

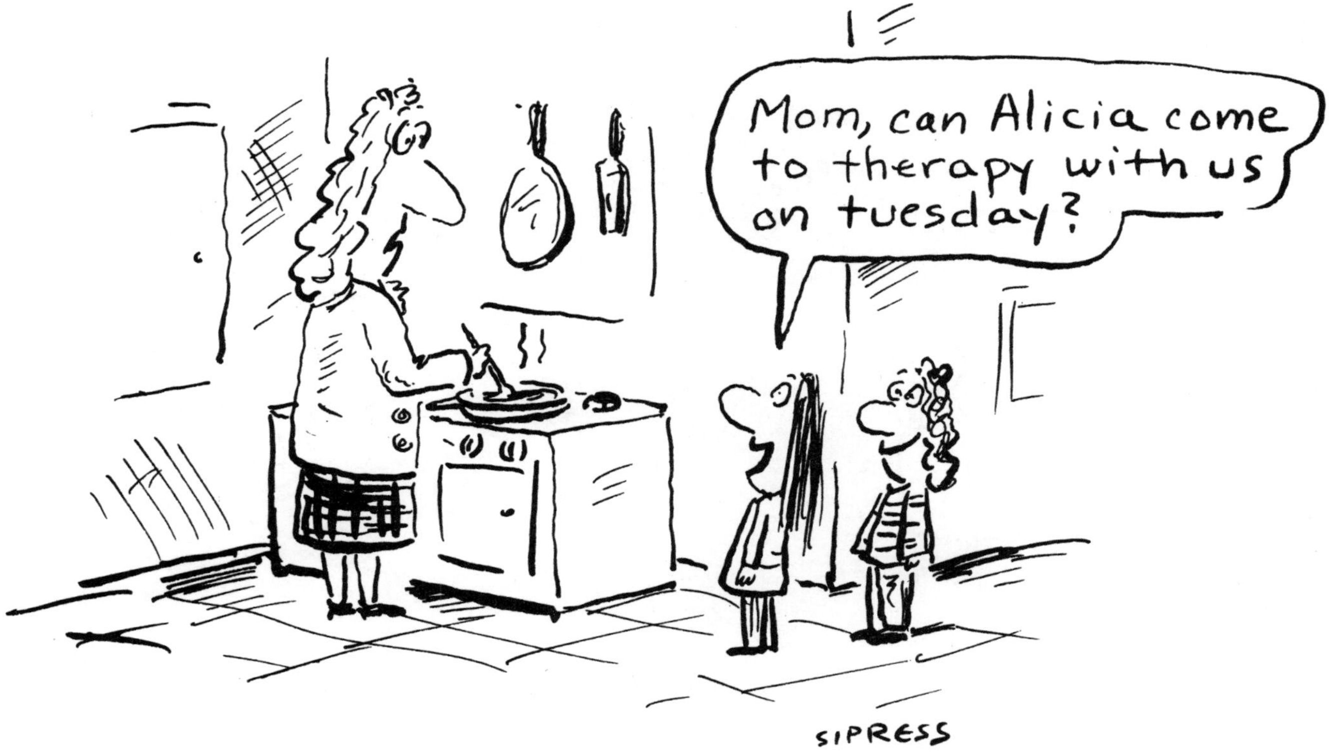
Mom, can Alicia come to therapy with us on tuesday?
SIPRESS

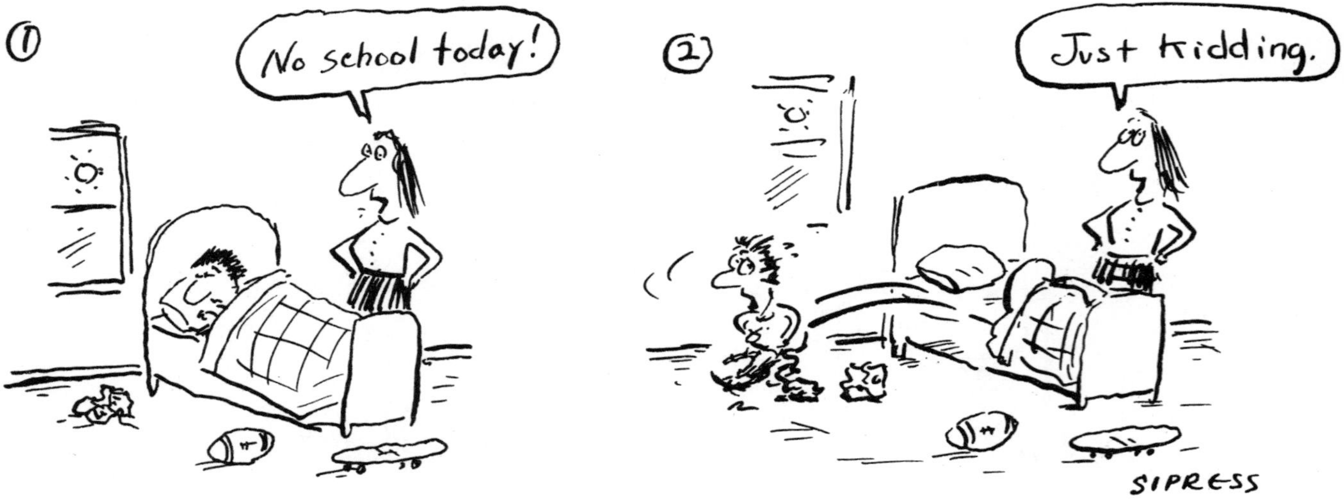
①
No school today!
②
Just kidding.
SIPRESS

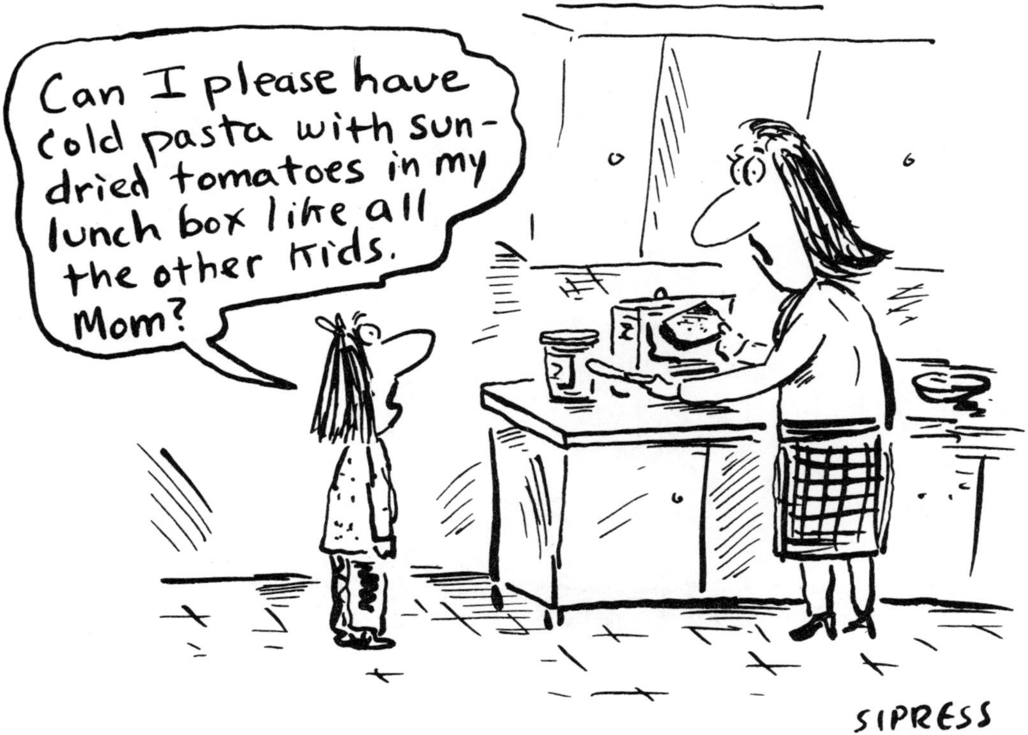
Can I please have cold pasta with sun-dried tomatoes in my lunch box like all the other kids, Mom?
SIPRESS

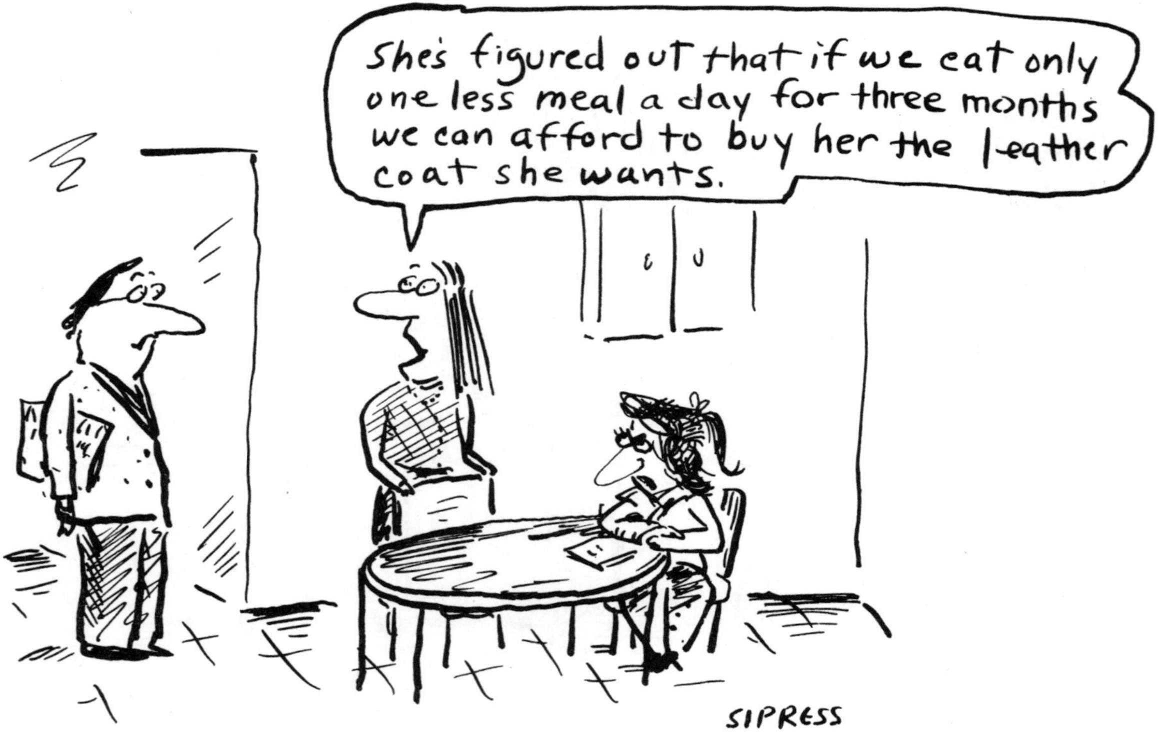
She's figured out that if we eat only one less meal a day for three months we can afford to buy her the leather coat she wants.
SIPRESS

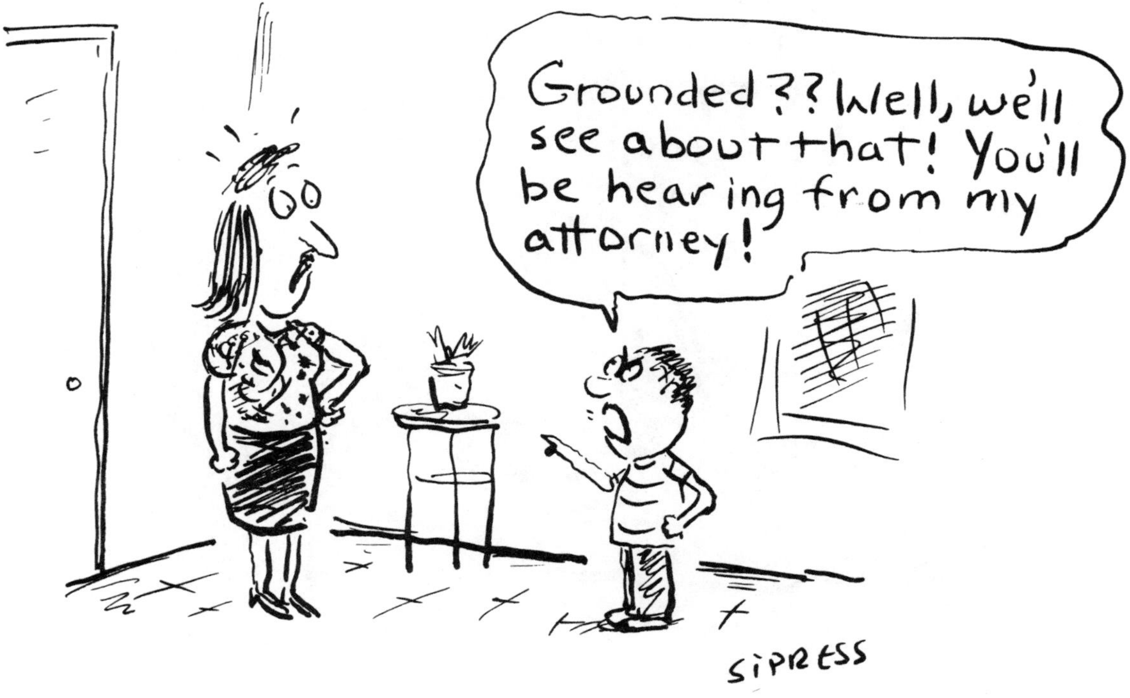
Grounded?? Well, we'll see about that! You'll be hearing from my attorney!
SIPRESS

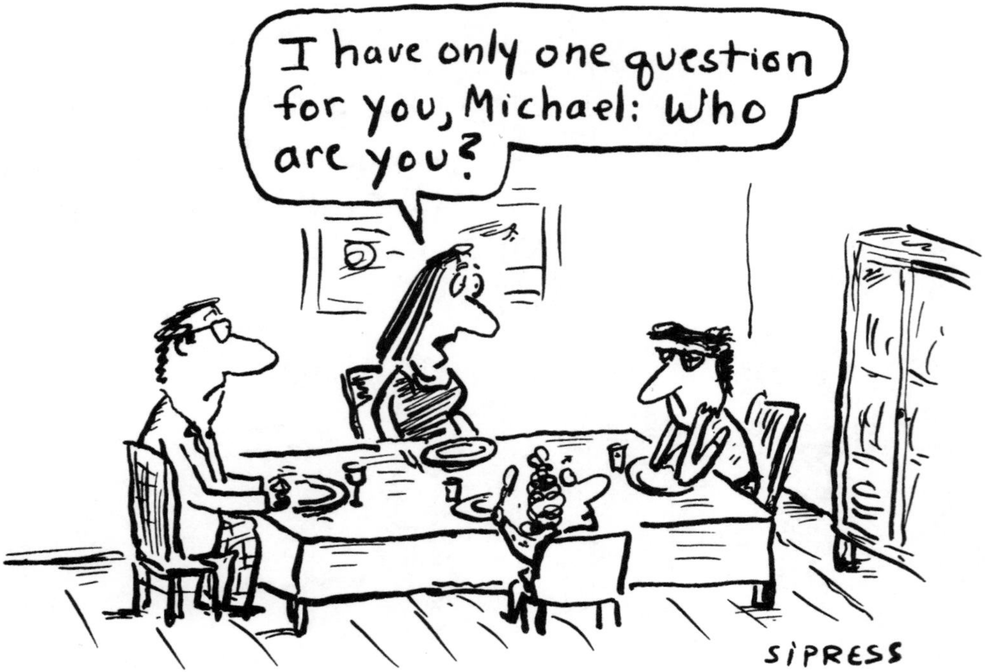
I have only one question for you, Michael: Who are you?
SIPRESS

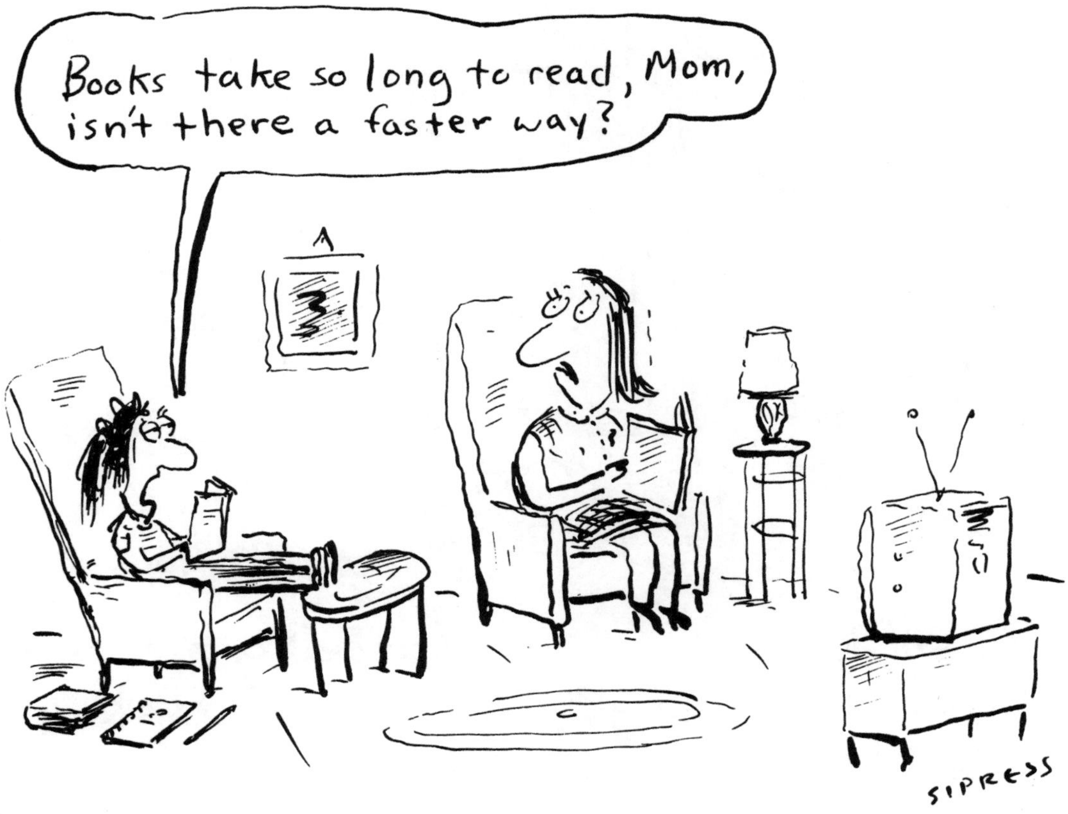
Books take so long to read, Mom, isn't there a faster way?
SIPRESS

I smoke because I'm stressed out! When you grow up and get stressed out, then you can smoke!

SIPRESS

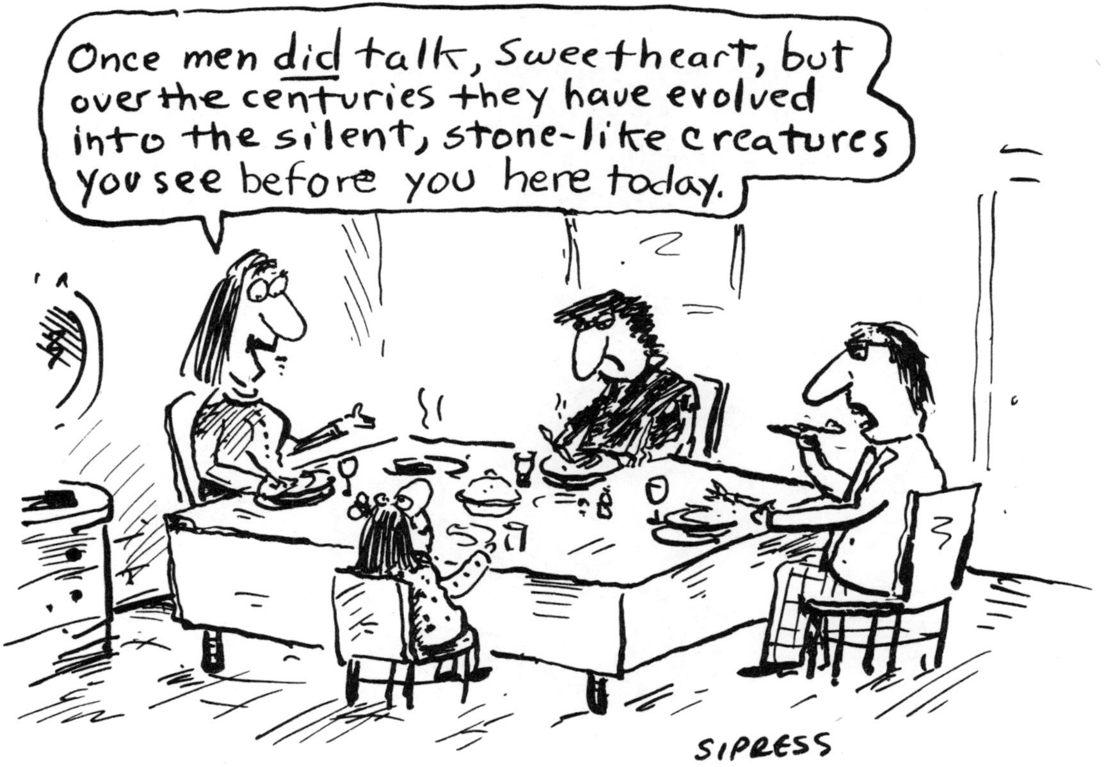
Once men did talk, sweetheart, but over the centuries they have evolved into the silent, stone-like creatures you see before you here today.
SIPRESS

So let me get this straight, Mom: Sex is healthy, natural, and lots of fun. But at the same time, it's scary, danger-ous, upsetting and potentially life-threatening.
SIPRESS

Well, here you are, Karen, both kids off to college and you're totally free! You can do whatever you want! How does it feel?
SIPRESS

I'm looking for a gift that says, "I love you, Mom, but I can't come visit on Mother's Day because I have other plans and my therapist says I need to set firm limits with you at this point in my life and only come see you when I really want to."
GIFTS
SIPRESS

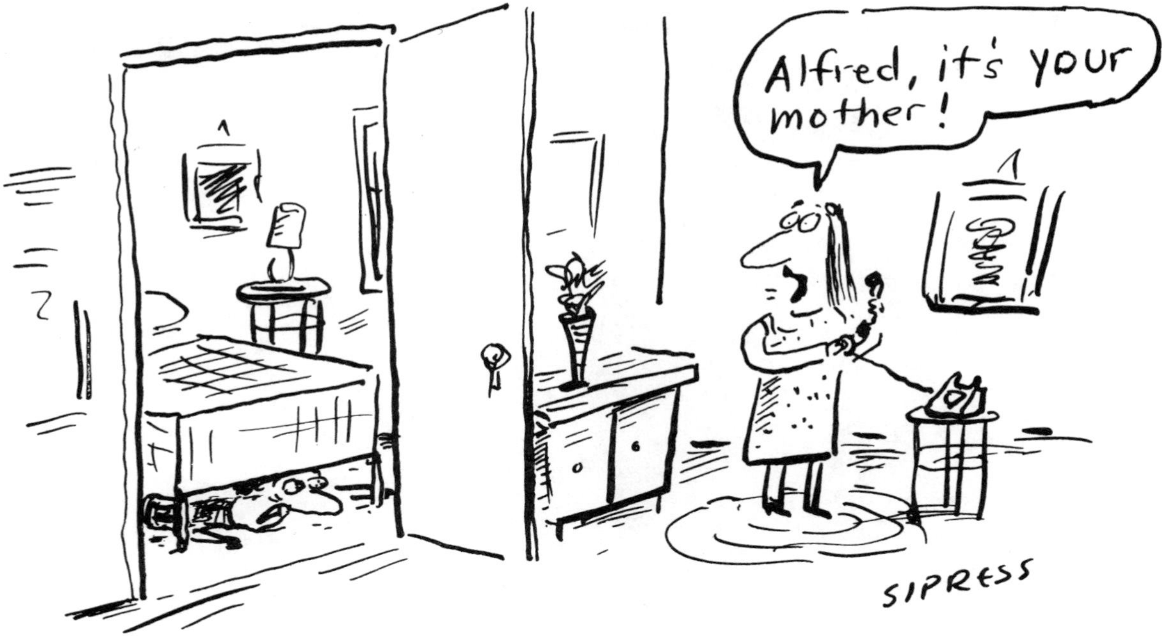
Alfred, it's your mother!
SIPRESS

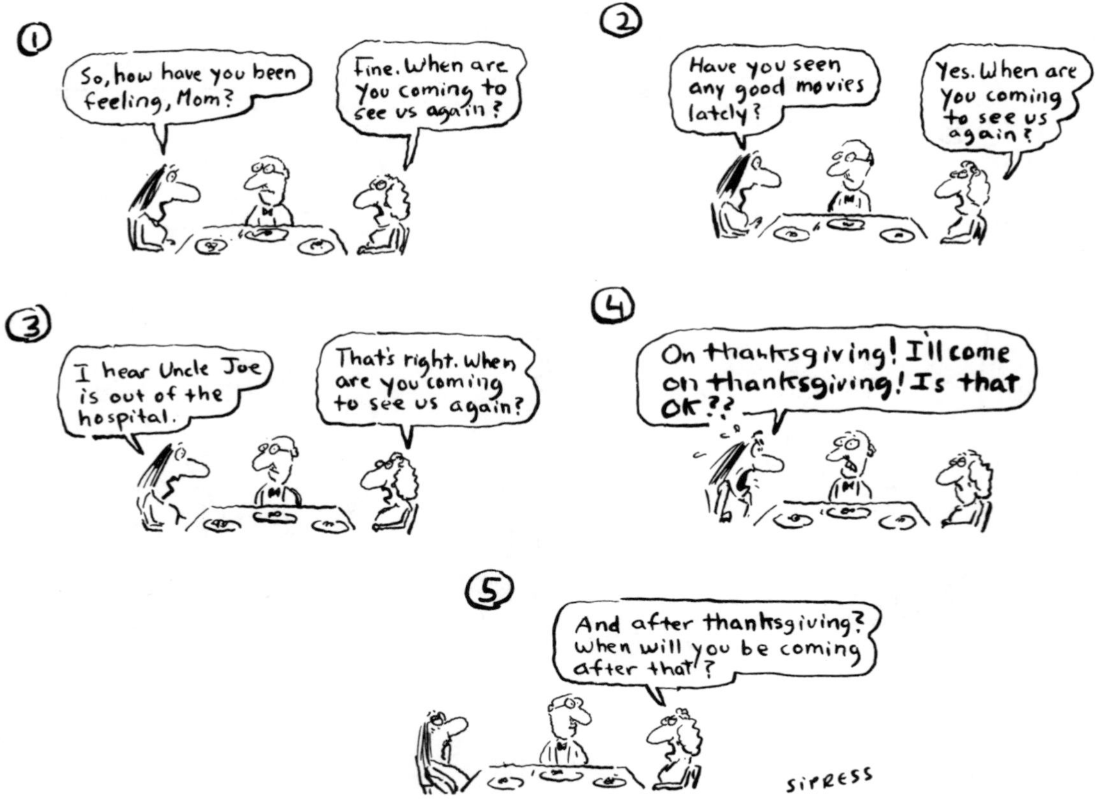
1
So, how have you been feeling, Mom?
Fine. When are you coming to see us again?
2
Have you seen any good movies lately?
Yes. When are you coming to see us again?
3
I hear Uncle Joe is out of the hospital.
That's right. When are you coming to see us again?
4
On thanksgiving! I'll come on thanksgiving! Is that OK??
5
And after thanksgiving? When will you be coming after that?
SIPRESS

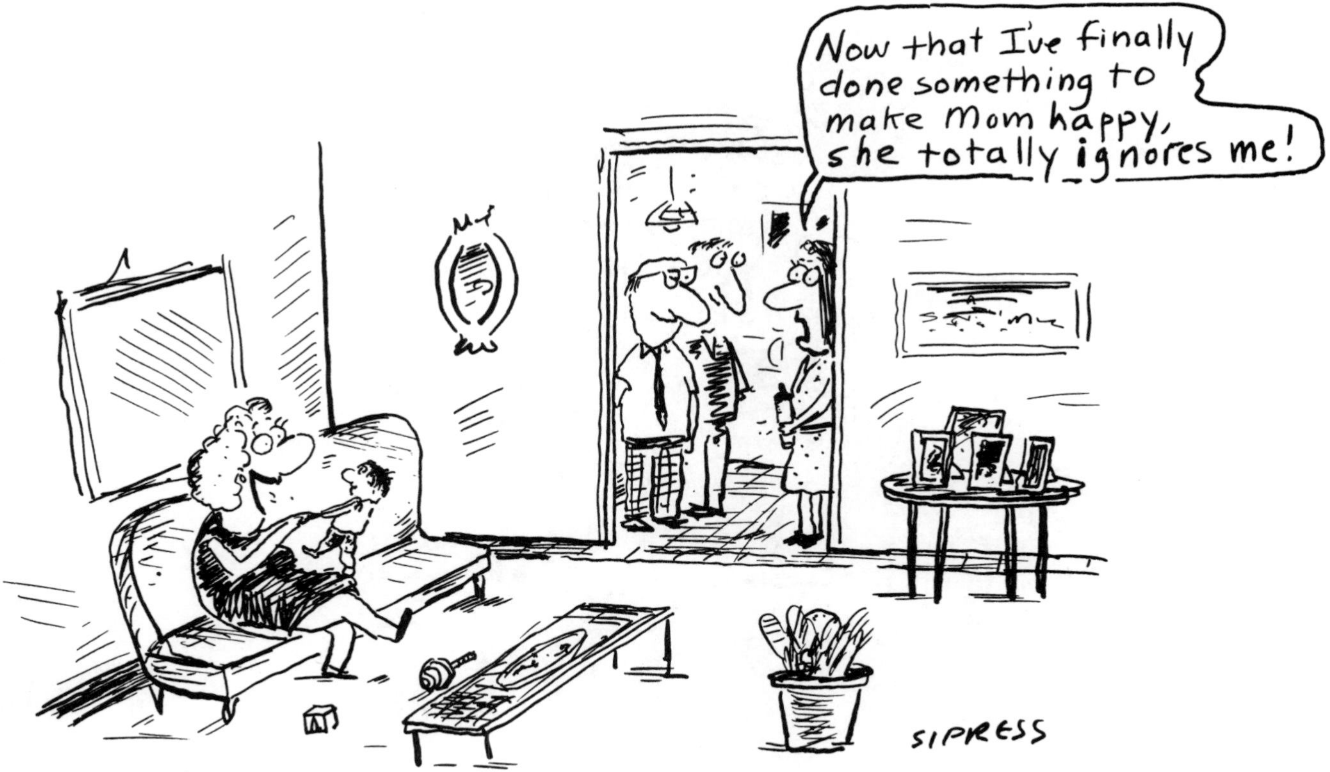
Now that I've finally done something to make Mom happy, she totally ignores me!
SIPRESS

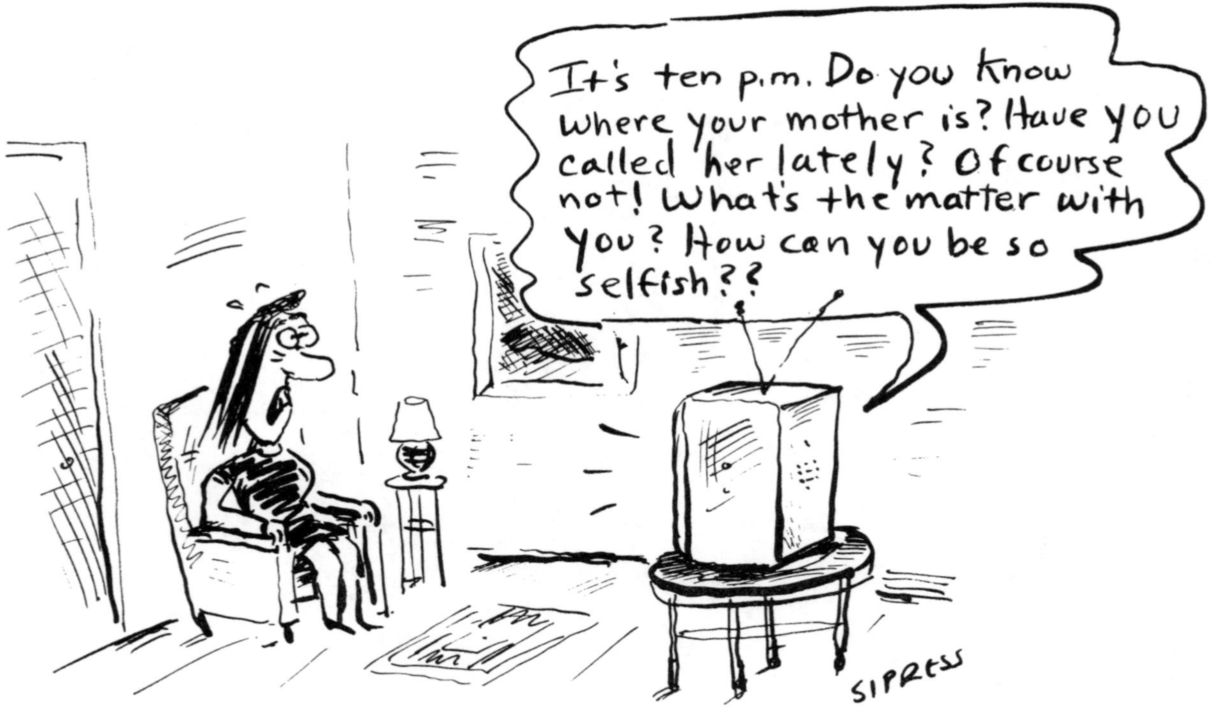
It's ten p.m. Do you know where your mother is? Have YOU called her lately? Of course not! What's the matter with you? How can you be so selfish??
SIPRESS

About the Author

David Sipress is the author of
It's a Mom's Life, It's a Dad's Life,
It's a Cat's Life, Sex, Love, and Other Problems,
and The Secret Life of Dogs. A cartoonist and sculptor,
he currently resides in New York City. His work
has appeared in Spy, Harper's, New Woman, Family Circle,
Psychology Today, and the Boston Phoenix.